9 12 $10 00

VOLTAIRE

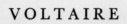

VOLTAIRE

*(From the plaster statuette in the possession of Sir Arthur Pinero,
made by Houdon as a preliminary study for the statue
now in the foyer of the Comédie Française)*

VOLTAIRE

BY

ANDRÉ MAUROIS

TRANSLATED FROM THE FRENCH

BY

HAMISH MILES

WITH A FRONTISPIECE

PETER DAVIES LIMITED

1932

First published in March 1932

Printed in Great Britain for PETER DAVIES LTD. by T. and A. CONSTABLE LTD. at the University Press, Edinburgh

CONTENTS

5

VOLTAIRE

6

I

THE BIRTH AND CHARACTER OF THE EIGHTEENTH CENTURY

THE reign of Louis XIV. of France was the lawful dictatorship of an intelligent statesman. It was a necessary dictatorship. Before it, the French nobility was a bellicose and undisciplined caste, whose factious wars made the country ungovernable. Personal quarrels were as fierce as those of parties. Between 1589 and 1607 seven thousand men met their death in duels. To the giant individuals of the Renaissance that force which was to become the modern State was a novelty, and one which they did not recognise. Richelieu curbed them momentarily, but during the young King's minority they surged up again, in all their headstrong valiance and wildness. The women themselves were amazons, prouder and fiercer than the men : Gaston d'Orléans addressed a letter to ' My Lady Countesses, marshals in the Army of my daughter against the Mazarin. . . .' To read the memoirs of Cardinal de Retz or of La Rochefoucauld, is to realise that an absolute master, and only an absolute master, could tame these heroic and dangerous prodigies.

What Richelieu had begun, Mazarin, and then Louis xiv., completed. The seventeenth century saw the defeat of the great feudal lords, that is to say, of the individual defying the State. Their defeat was accompanied by a revolution in literature and in high society. The rude soldiers of the civil wars learned to live in drawing-rooms. Round Louis xiv. there came into being a Court where the individual was polished by the spirit of society. The horseman became the cavalier ; swords changed from weapons to ornaments. The sole concern of these soldiers retired in their prime was love-making. Women were omnipotent, and the analysis of the feelings which they inspired or experienced became almost the sole theme of conversation or of writing. To express the finest shades, the language acquired precision, abstraction, and purity. The classic spirit was born.

At least two periods must be distinguished in the history of the classic spirit. During the first, that of Corneille, Molière, La Rochefoucauld, and Mme. de Sévigné, the classic spirit is a perfection of form imposed upon strength of feelings. A great classic is not an insensitive creature ; he has the same passions as a great romantic. But ' he is shaped by the habit of speaking, writing, and thinking in the midst of a drawing-room assemblage.' The choice of words has lightness of texture. The writer avoids technicalities, pedantries or crudities, which are painful or tiresome in agreeable company. He strives for clarity and swiftness, and expresses his personal sufferings in the form of general maxims rather than lyrical outpourings, because violence is in bad taste. But there are outcrops of passion showing through the transparence of the maxims, and awareness of their existence of that underlying passion gives the great classics their own beauty.

After forty or fifty years the classic spirit degenerates. The surface remains chaste and polished, but no longer hides anything underneath. Taste becomes constricted ; contact with reality is broken by the fear of the concrete word. The tragedies of Crébillon and Voltaire succeed those of Racine. We no longer have an heroic nobility submitting to the life of the salon, but a drawing-room nobility vainly striving to summon up heroic sentiments. Love becomes libertine. ' Married life is topsy-turvy and gallantry universal.' Now, cynicism has at all times been suicidal for the ruling classes. And on the ruins of the collapsed nobility there appears a critical, ironic bourgeoisie, whose scoffing is backed up by a section of the Court chafing against the retirement to which Louis XIV. condemned them. Young nobles dream of a neo-feudal movement, of an aristocratic and popular reaction, rather as the youthful English conservatives of Disraeli's ' Young England ' did later ; whence La Fayette, the night of the Fourth of August 1789, and then the Terror. The death of Louis XIV., a minor's reign, the regency of a disillusioned libertine, open the floodgates of a critical and seditious movement which is to culminate, seventy-five years later, in the French Revolution.

The other deep current of the epoch is the

shaping of modern science, the mathematical
sciences, or those derived from mathematics
(astronomy, mechanics, optics), being the
first to develop. After Copernicus, Galileo,
and Descartes, reasoning processes apparently
enable men to calculate and foretell the move-
ments of stars, the fall of a body, the course of
a beam of light. The human mind is intoxicated by this new power. Reason appears as
omnipotent. Reason is expected to explain
the passions, and politics, and God. An abstract
vocabulary, its elements handled like algebraic
signs, gives moralists and philosophers the idea
that by pure reason they can solve all problems.
Spinoza, in his *Ethics*, has already put metaphysics into theorems, corollaries, and scholia.
In the eighteenth century the French and
English philosophers would try to make logical
reasoning take the place of instinct and tradition in the conduct of life.

They are perhaps beginning to catch
glimpses of what experimental science will be,
but as yet they are far from the strict method,
the humble subservience to facts, which during
the next two centuries are to bring about the
shattering advance of physics and chemistry.

But science has already transformed the con-
ception of the world held by thinking men.
Instead of seeing therein a simple drama
staged by a divine Providence, they discern the
infinitely complex play of countless small
forces. Ceasing to regard himself as the
centre of all things, man sees himself as a
minute animal in a tiny parish of the universe. Religion is enfeebled by such modes of
thought, just as the monarchy is enfeebled by
the existence of a critical bourgeoisie and a
discontented nobility. The whole scaffolding
which upheld seventeenth-century France is
giving way.

One of the Frenchmen who was most vigorous in the bending and breaking of that
scaffolding was a bourgeois, the son of a notary
named Arouet, who numbered amongst his
clients several noble families, amongst them
that of the Duc de Saint-Simon.

II

CHILDHOOD AND EDUCATION

On November 22nd, 1694, a sickly infant was baptized in Paris—François-Marie Arouet. Later he rebaptized himself Voltaire, a name which according to some came from a small family property, and others affirmed to be an anagram on the words 'Arouet le Jeune.' And the word Voltaire can indeed be formed from 'Arouet L.J.' if U is taken as V and J as I. But anagram-hunters find their game in every covert, even Bacon in Shakespeare.

We should bear in mind the weakness of Voltaire at his birth; he was to make a weapon of his frailness. As a matter of fact he was immediately very much alive, both in mind and body. At the age of three his godfather, the libertine Abbé de Châteauneuf, made him recite the *Fables* of La Fontaine and an agnostic poem entitled the *Mosaïde*, wherein all religions were denounced:

All the world argues—Papists, Siamese :
'*Tis black*, cry those, and then '*Tis white*, cry these . . .

O Folly most fanatical
And vain :
Men view what's most fantastical
As plain !

' He is only three and he knows the whole of
the *Mosaïde* by heart,' boasted Châteauneuf
to his old friend Ninon de Lenclos, beloved
of three generations. From him Voltaire
learned to compose French verses and to hate
bigots. The elder son of the notary Arouet
was a Jansenist, devout and straitlaced in his
faith. In the violence of Voltaire's feelings
about religious subjects there was doubtless
an element of hostility towards an intolerable
elder.

At ten he was sent to the College of Louis-le-
Grand, a Jesuit institution. The Jesuits formed
him in their own image. They nourished their
pupils on Latin and rhetoric, imbuing them
with respect for the ancient styles—the epic, the
tragedy, and the dialogue. Attaching great
importance to form and to brilliance of tone,
they imparted the wisdom of this world. Their
pupil, François-Marie Arouet, fitted in with

14

them perfectly. Making a pretext of his weak health to escape from games in the hours of recreation, he spent those times in showering questions on Fathers Tournemine and Porée. When his companions laughed at his over-studious life he answered : ' Everyone has his own way of jumping and amusing himself.'

The child was curious about everything. Never had the Jesuits of Louis-le-Grand found so precociously universal a mind. The kindly Father Porée, a man ' full of candour and merit,' talked politics with him, and remarked affectionately that the boy ' enjoyed weighing in his little scales the great interests of Europe.' In other directions this schoolboy statesman remained a child, and would play tricks on his masters. The school stoves were only lighted when the holy-water stoup in the chapel froze. But Arouet could not stand cold, so he used to gather icicles in the courtyard and secretly throw them into the stoup. That trick was an exact prefiguration of his destiny.

The fondness of the Jesuits for fine accomplishment made them wholeheartedly fond of an infant prodigy who, at twelve years old, could write elegant and flowing verses with the

utmost ease. They took it upon themselves
to pass his epigrams round. One of them was
also shown by Châteauneuf to Ninon, and the
beautiful octogenarian asked to have its author
brought to see her. The Abbé brought his
godson. Questioning him about the Jansenist
disputes, she found him witty and forthright,
and when she died bequeathed him a small
sum to buy books.

A famous and erudite courtesan, a free-
living Abbé, the Jesuits—this education of
Voltaire's is sufficient explanation of why he
so perfectly represented his time. It has been
said that the eighteenth century was Voltaire's
century, as the seventeenth had been that of
Louis xiv. This is quite true. In the century
of a critical bourgeoisie, Voltaire was a critical
bourgeois ; in a century of religious bickerings,
he was at once very well-informed about theological disputes, curious about their objects,
and anti-religious ; in a century of classicism
he was a classic, inheritor of the disciplines of
the preceding reign ; in a century of budding
science he was, not a savant, but a cultured
amateur with a wonderful gift for popularising
knowledge. On leaving college he was so

fully aware of his powers that when his father suggested his taking up a profession, he answered : ' I want none but that of man of letters.'

The notary Arouet, who had meanwhile acquired by purchase an official legal post, would have liked to make his son a lawyer. But how could one make a law-student of a youth who had no respect for anything ? Vainly he was told of the respect attached to the magistracy : ' Tell my father that I want no consideration that is bought and sold ; I can make one for myself that will cost nothing.' From the age of twenty, at first thanks to Châteauneuf, but then rapidly by the charm of his wit, he mingled socially with men of the highest rank. He lived in the luxurious and dissipated society which surrounded the aged poet Chaulieu. He was presented to the Prince de Conti and the Duc de Vendôme. He corrected the verses written by fashionable ladies —which is one way of winning their favour when one has more wits than vigour. He wrote a tragedy—*Œdipe*, which he believed to be a novelty because, like the Greek tragedies, it contained ' choruses and no love.' The ad-

miration of his coterie intoxicated him.
Through satires, epigrams, and witty remarks,
he began to cultivate the gentle art of making
enemies. He treated as equals the noble per-
sonages who had become his friends. ' Are
we all princes here, or all poets ? ' he asked
them once when he sat down at table. He
had not yet experienced the moments of
recurrent pride, the intermittent harshness
of the Great.

He would have experienced them in his
early twenties had not his godfather Châteauneuf, fortunately for him, been appointed
ambassador to Holland. Thither he took the
lad as page. A page, the youthful Arouet ?
In his youthfulness, his elegant lyrical turn,
his love verses, he was a page. But an un-
sentimental one, and devilish serious underneath all his wildness. Rather frail for love,
but sturdy for work. . . . A page ? Perhaps :
but more of a novice, the novice of a new
religion which would combat fanaticism, pend-
ing the day when it would become fanatical
itself.

III

COMEDIES

THE page opened his sojourn in the Low
Countries as Cherubino should: he fell in love.
There was a certain Mme. Dunoyer living at
The Hague, rather a dangerous lady, a French
Protestant who had left her husband, carried
off her daughters, and taken refuge in Holland,
where she lived by selling scurrilous verses and
satires against respectable people. Voltaire
saw her and despised her, but under her roof
he found a quite young girl, Olympe by name,
whom he was soon calling Pimpette. 'Yes,
my dear Pimpette, I shall love you always.
The most faithless lovers say as much, but
their love is not founded as mine on a perfection of esteem. I love your virtue no less than
your person.'

Notwithstanding such respect, Mme.
Dunoyer took umbrage at the assiduities of the
page, and complained to Châteauneuf, who

put Voltaire under open arrest. He kept
bounds in the daytime, but broke them by
night to visit his mistress. 'There is nothing,
my dear Pimpette, which I would not risk for
you. You deserve much more.' And then,
when he was not allowed out any longer, he
sent her his clothes so that she could dress as
a cavalier and visit him—which she did.

> At last I've seen you, charmer of my heart,
> To-day a cavalier by mummer's art !
> Methought I saw fair Venus' self for sure,
> Wearing the very figure of Amour. . . .

The ambassador was vexed, dreading the
mischievous journalist of a mother, and sent
Voltaire back to Paris.

There he was coldly received by the notary.
As a father, Arouet had no luck. His elder
son, more and more Jansenist, was becoming
positively inhuman in his devoutness. His
younger son was proving only too human. 'My
sons are a pair of madmen,' he used to say,
' one in prose and t'other in verse.' In those
days a father had little difficulty in obtaining
from the government an order entitling him
to confine or to exile his children. M. Arouet
procured one. Voltaire went into hiding, and

with his usual activity immediately began pulling countless strings to pacify his father and to arrange the abduction of his mistress.

He had conceived the admirable idea of enlisting the support of the Jesuits, and of having Pimpette removed by French bishops. ' In point of fact,' he said, ' Mlle. Dunoyer is a Protestant. She is kept at The Hague against her will, in heresy, by a cruel mother. She only asks to become a Catholic in order to marry me, and if she is carried off she will recant.' Father Tournemine, his former master at Louis-le-Grand, was very fond of young Arouet, and undertook to pass on this story to Father Letellier, another Jesuit who was also confessor to the King, and so all-powerful. It looked as if the wild enterprise must be successful ; but the Ambassador Châteauneuf quashed it by writing that the anger of the Dutch government would be aroused. There was nothing left for Voltaire but to make peace with his father. To do so, he had to promise to resume the study of law, and to enter the office of a *procureur*. He did not stay there long.

In 1715 Louis XIV. died. The reign of all

the glories ended dismally. The last wars had not favoured France ; the finances were in sorry plight ; and consciences had been vexed for fifty years by the quarrels round Jansenism. In 1641 Rome had condemned a book by Jansenius, Bishop of Ypres, which maintained that God can command things of the faithful which are impossible to them because the necessary grace is lacking in them. Over this question of efficacious grace the whole of France was cleft asunder. Jansenists had been persecuted by Jesuits. Their monastic house of Port-Royal had been razed, their adherents sent to the Bastille. Towards the close of the reign, after seeming to settle down, the quarrel suddenly revived, the occasion being a book by Father Quesnel, which Rome had at first regarded as excellent but had later discovered to be Jansenist, and was condemned by the Pope in the Bull styled *Unigenitus*. Once again France was split into two religious camps, and those who refused to accept the Bull were imprisoned by *lettre de cachet*. The King's confessor, Letellier, was blamed for these persecutions and also the King himself. In fine, confusion seized the land.

For all which reasons the old sovereign was
mourned by none. The young King, as Saint-
Simon remarks, was not old enough. The
new Regent, the Duc d'Orléans, ' was not his
paid mourner.' Mme. de Maintenon ' was
weary of the King, and was at her wits' ends
to amuse him.' The Duc du Maine and the
other bastard princes, hoping for omnipotence,
displayed barbaric joy. Court and ministers
alike had the sense of being freed from an intolerable yoke. ' Paris breathed again in the
hope of some liberty and the joy of seeing
an end to the sway which so many people
abused.' The common people, believing themselves crushed by taxation, hoped, wrongly
as always, that a new regime would cure
their woes. On the day of the funeral
ceremonies drinking-booths were set up along
the road to Saint-Denis. Voltaire went to
see the spectacle and observed the crowd
drunk with wine and jubilation. It left him
pensive.

In that first moment of liberty men believed
they could speak their minds about everything.
Pamphlets on the old regime pullulated. Voltaire joined in, and others which were not

from his pen were attributed to him. The
new Regent, Philippe d'Orléans, was a man
of no ill-will. ' He was very fond of liberty,'
said Saint-Simon, ' for others as much as for
himself. He once upheld England to me as a
country where there was neither exile nor
lettres de cachet.' But that did not prevent him
from signing one consigning young Voltaire
to the Bastille, where he left him for over a
year. It was a stern punishment for a few
mischievous verses, and was bound to rouse
strong depths of feeling and useful reflections
on the forms of justice, in the mind of a young
man of lively spirit suddenly enclosed between
four walls. One imagines him pacing up and
down all day, sharpening harsh and satisfying
phrases, and dreaming of the English constitution and *Habeas Corpus.*

In the Bastille, Voltaire worked. His wish
was to become the great epic poet of France.
In his prison he composed the first cantos of a
long poem on Henri IV., the *Henriade*, which
gave splendid openings for pleas against
intolerance :

> That hero, sovereign of France, I sing,
> By rights of conquest and of birth her King.

Arma virumque cano. . . . It began like the *Æneid* ; which was all very well in the *Æneid*, but hardly in a poem written in 1723. The first canto contained at least one line which remained famous :

Who shines subservient, rising, is eclips'd . . .

and many others which were often quoted in the time of the Revolution but are now forgotten. The Bastille itself was described :

Palace of vengeance, dark and bodeful pile,
Where languish side by side the pure, the vile.

In the end, after eighteen months of confinement, Voltaire was able to leave the fortress. A few days later he saw the Regent, who received him with a laugh, for he was not a man of ill-will and bore no rancour towards a young man whom he had imprisoned for eighteen months because of a song. 'Monseigneur,' Voltaire said to him. 'I should be well pleased if His Majesty deigned to provide for my keep, but I beg Your Highness to make no further provision for my lodging.'

It was customary to follow up a departure from the Bastille with a short and becoming exile. The Duc de Béthune invited Voltaire to spend his in his château of Sully. Imprisonment had damaged his health and the country air would do him good. He was very happy at Sully, where he became the lover of a young lady named Mlle. de Livry, who planned a career in the theatre for herself and bade him write parts for her.

IV

TRAGEDIES

A MADNESS lay over France. All restraint had passed with the giant shade of the old King. Great quarrels raged round petty causes. The men of letters were divided by Homer, and churchmen by the Bull *Unigenitus*. The spirit of irreligion had been strong enough under the previous reign ; it now dared to flaunt itself. There was a complete cynicism in morals. The Regent himself was accused of incest with his daughter, the Duchesse de Berry, and every one laughed. Crimes were merely a topic for the rhymesters. The theatres were full. 'Everything was turned to gaiety and jesting ; the spirit was the same as in the time of the Fronde, not far from civil war.'

In this singing, rebellious Paris, Voltaire was to present his *Œdipe*. This bad tragedy was a great event. The author was known to belong to the opposition camp, to have been sent to the Bastille, and indeed to be only lately freed. His play was said to be hostile to the priesthood, even to religion, and he was supposed to have depicted the incest of Œdipus only to strike at that of the Regent. The public came in throngs ; and they were not disappointed. *Œdipe* was rather a common-place tragedy, an exercise in rhetoric by one of Father Porée's bright pupils, a skilful if unconscious pastiche of Racine ; but the Parisians of 1718 were looking less for the King of Thebes than for the Regent of France, less for the high priest than for the French bishops. Platitudes were words of daring in their ears.

Trust only in ourselves—see all with our own eyes :
From that our tripods, oracles, and Gods shall rise.

A bad couplet, but it indicated beyond a doubt that experimental science was winning against the revelations of the so-called sacred writings.

Our priests are ne'er what foolish men have ever said :
Of our credulity is all their science made.

The ' foolish ' people, weary of the King's confessor, the Bull *Unigenitus*, and sentences for sacrilege, clapped their hands. They recked little of the young poet's rusty arsenal of highflown poetic phrases ; *Œdipe* was a rebels' play at a time of rebellion. It was a triumph.

The Regent, a wit in his way, came in person to see the fashionable tragedy ; his daughter was seen at the theatre, and with crowning effrontery Voltaire dedicated his play to the Duchesse d'Orléans. Women paid court to him ; men praised him ; writers envied him. He pirouetted, loved, worked, attacked, counter-attacked. Cabals were formed against him. A terrific poem appeared anonymously, aimed against the Regent—the *Philippiques*. Voltaire was accused of being its author. He was not, but how could he prove it ? Already a chorus of his enemies was advising the Regent to send him back to the Bastille, but Philippe d'Orléans had taken a fancy to this lively young man and was kind enough to exile him. Voltaire left Paris in the midst of a violent thunderstorm. Looking up at the clouds, the lightning, the whole celestial turmoil, he made one remark : ' The Kingdom of Heaven must have sunk into a Regency.'

Once more he found a haven at Sully. Mlle. de Livry was there, and he spent the period of his disgrace in writing a tragedy for her, entitled *Artémire*. Shortly afterwards it was put on the stage, and this ' hapless queen ' was hissed. Suddenly interrupting his exile, Voltaire made a sally to the theatre in defence of his play and its interpreter, but the cabal was powerful. Young though he was, he had made determined enemies : a certain Abbé Desfontaines by doing him a favour, and the poet Jean-Baptiste Rousseau by adding some reservations to his praises. All his ' first nights ' caused an uproar. When he presented his Jewish tragedy, *Mariamne*, on the eve of Twelfth Night, at the moment when Mariamne, Herod's wife, was quaffing a poisoned goblet, a humorist in the pit called out : ' The Queen drinks ! ' After which the end of the play could never be heard. But what did it matter to Voltaire ? He felt himself supported by his noble friends. A check sent him scurrying to the Duc de Béthune at Sully, or to Lord Bolingbroke's at Le Source, near Orleans (Bolingbroke was his first English friend), or to the Maréchale de Villars at

Vaux (she permitted him to be her lover), or to Maisons, with the Président de Maisons. And everywhere he was rhyming, dancing, reading. He made jokes and every one laughed. He read plays and every one wept. In fine, he thought he was happy.

The awakening was abrupt and painful. One day at the Duc de Sully's, the self-assurance of this young man became annoying to the Chevalier de Rohan-Chabot, a rather unworthy scion of a great house. 'Who is this young man,' said M. de Rohan-Chabot, 'who talks so loud when he contradicts me?'— 'Sir,' replied Voltaire, 'he is a man who does not drag a great name behind him, but does honour to the one he bears!' The Chevalier left the table, and the Duc de Sully remarked to Voltaire: 'We are glad you have rid us of him.'

A few days later Voltaire was at the Duc de Sully's when he was asked to go down to the door of the mansion. Coming down, he saw a hackney carriage, in which were two men who asked him to come to the door. Trustingly he went over, and as soon as he got near the carriage they caught hold of him and be-

laboured him with sticks over the shoulders.
The Chevalier was a little way ahead in his
own carriage, observing the episode. ' Don't
hit his head ! ' he cried. ' Something good
might come out of that ! ' The people who had
gathered round shouted : ' Oh, the fine gentleman that he is ! ' And Voltaire went up again
to the Duc de Sully, battered about, his clothes
in disorder, begging his noble friends to come
with him to the guardians of law and order.
The Duc and his friends laughed, and would
do nothing of the sort. After all, it was a
Rohan who had thrashed a poet. It was a
regrettable adventure, but one in conformity
with the ordering of the world.

Ordinarily Voltaire was more courageous in
mind than in body, but he had been cut to the
quick and he wanted vengeance. He took
lessons from a fencing-master, declaring everywhere that he was going to provoke M. de
Rohan-Chabot, with the result that the Rohans
took fright and obtained an order for the
Bastille for this thin-skinned groundling. He
had been beaten, then ; he had not been able
to secure justice, and it was himself whom
they proposed to imprison. Yes, Regency

France was a gay and charming country, but not easily habitable for a free man. This time Voltaire remained in the Bastille for only a few days. The Minister Maurepas, perhaps ashamed, let him out with a request to leave the country.

The incident was important because it succeeded in finally turning Voltaire into a man of the opposition camp. To the Rohan affair he certainly owed some part of his genius. He now had passions. The incest of Œdipus, the love of Mariamne, the exploits of Henri IV., and even Pimpette's travesties, were cold themes which could only inspire cold poems. But the folly of the world, its injustices, the malice of men, the silence of God—here were strong feelings from which some day a masterpiece would surge up.

V

VOLTAIRE IN ENGLAND

On leaving the Bastille, he decided to cross to England. That nation, with an elected parliament and knowing nothing of *lettres de cachet*, was fashionable amongst philosophers. ' I know,' wrote Voltaire to a friend when he left, ' that it is a country where the arts are all honoured and rewarded, where there are differences of condition, but none other betwixt men save that of merit. It is a country where men think freely and nobly, unhampered by any servile fear.' He knew a few words of English. Horace Walpole, the English ambassador in Paris, gave him letters of introduction to several people. Besides, he had an influential friend in London in Lord Bolingbroke, whom he had known in France in the days when Bolingbroke, the lover and then the husband of a Frenchwoman, Mme. de Villette, had bought a château near Orleans. Bolingbroke and his lady had listened to his reading of the *Henriade*, then in manuscript, and praised it. Thanks to them Voltaire had hopes of getting to know the English men of letters and to find in London the fashionable life he was so fond of. Above all, he wanted peace and freedom of thought ; and from British tolerance he expected both.

It was believed in France at that time that England was not a religious country. ' No religion in England,' wrote Montesquieu. ' If anyone mentions religion, everybody begins to laugh.' This was true only of quite a small number of writers and great noblemen. But certainly the Anglican Church was more tolerant than the Jansenist Parlements of Paris. English churchmen ' insisted on the reasonable character of Christianity, and the miracles reported in the Bible were regarded as the historical proofs of a system which could be accepted by the common sense of every age.' In fact, following the great English tradition, a compromise was accepted : men were religious without being fanatical, philosophers without being subversive. Even the Nonconformists had become less zealous. ' The Quakers were spiritually appeased and economically pros-

perous.' It was not till later, in Wesley's time,
that religion found a new emotional force, until
the French Revolution transformed it again in
England into a political and conservative force.

Arrived in London, Voltaire could not find
' Milord Bolingbroke,' who, as a matter of fact,
throughout his stay, was very suspicious of his
' verbiage ' and wondered whether he were not
a French political agent.   On the other hand,
the poet was made welcome at Wandsworth, a
few miles out of London, by a merchant named
Falkener, in whose house he settled down and
to whom he dedicated his tragedy of *Zaïre* in
1733—' To Mr. Falkener, English merchant.
You are an Englishman, my dear friend, and I
was born in France ; but lovers of the arts are
fellow-citizens. . . . Accordingly, I offer you
this tragedy as to my own compatriot in letters
and as to my intimate friend. . . . At the same
time I rejoice in the opportunity of telling my
own country in what light men of business are
regarded in yours, and in what esteem England
can hold a calling which makes the greatness of
the State.'   It was the first time that a French
tragedy had been dedicated to a merchant : it
seemed extraordinarily daring.

Little is known of Voltaire's stay in London. It is known that he gave his address as that of Bolingbroke, and that he stayed for a long time in the country with Lord Peterborough, where, it is said, he spent three months with Swift. Thanks to Falkener he saw something of the mercantile world, and he admired its power and its authority in Parliament, which flattered his own bourgeois pride. It was in this company that he acquired a liking for business, in which he was to become so successful. His first venture was the subscribing of an English edition of his poem, the *Henriade*, in a luxurious quarto edition and a limited printing. He wrote to Swift, asking him to use his influence in Ireland to secure a few subscribers to the *Henriade*, which was ready, but failing a little more help, had not yet appeared : the price was but a guinea, payable in advance. The publication was a great success, the edition being entirely subscribed.

At Bolingbroke's he met the half-republican conservatives who then formed that Tory Democracy which Disraeli was later to revive, and he met the great writers of the time. Swift and Voltaire were born to mutual understanding and admiration. *Gulliver's Travels* had been published a few years before (1726), and Voltaire busied himself with obtaining its translation into French : ' the Rabelais of England,' he said, ' but a Rabelais without the rubbish, and the book would be amusing in itself, by reason of the singular imaginings which fill it, and by its lightness of style, quite apart from the satire of the human race.' He was less taken with the second volume : ' You will find in the same parcel the second volume of Mr. Gulliver,' he wrote, in English. ' That continuate series of new fangles, follies, of fairy tales, of wild inventions, pall at last upon our taste. Nothing unnatural may please long. It is for this reason that commonly the second parts of romances are so insipid.' For the same reason, no doubt, Voltaire never wrote a sequel to *Candide*—for which he should be praised.

He also saw Pope, Congreve (who, a typical English man of letters, refused to let Voltaire call him a poet, saying that his only wish was to be a private gentleman), and Gay, who showed him the *Beggar's Opera* before its public performance. He frequented the Rainbow Tavern, and often visited the playhouses, where he acquired a greater familiarity with Shakespeare than most Frenchmen of the time had. He also enjoyed visiting the meetings of Quakers or the conventicles of sectaries. Legend has it that he was chased in the street by a mob one day because his foreign dress annoyed them, and that he placated his assailants by mounting on a bench and saying to them : ' My brave Englishmen, am I not luckless enough already, not to have been born one of yourselves ? ' Whereupon he was cheered three times three, and carried home in triumph on the shoulders of those who had hooted him.

Naturally he profited by his sojourn in England to read the English philosophers, especially ' Mister Loke.' In 1727 he witnessed the burial of Newton, and was amazed by the magnificent honours paid to scientific genius. The body, exposed by torchlight on a State bed, was borne to Westminster Abbey, followed by a long procession, including the Lord Chancellor and Ministers of the Crown. The ceremony contrasted strongly with the Bastille and the belabourings of chevaliers.

In later years he withdrew some of his

enthusiasm : ' I thought in my young days that Newton's fortune was made by his outstanding merit. I had imagined that the Court and City of London had acclaimed him as Master of the Mint of the realm. Not at all. Isaac Newton had an agreeable niece, named Mrs. Conduit. She took the fancy of Halifax, the Lord High Treasurer. The infinitesimal calculus and gravitation would have availed him naught had it not been for a pretty niece.'

It is not known exactly why or when he left England, but during the first months of 1729 he was in France. At first he remained in hiding, stopping at Saint-Germain and lodging with a wigmaker. From there he wrote ' to the Vizier Maurepas, asking leave to trail his chains in Paris.'

VI

SUCCESSES AND PERSECUTIONS

VOLTAIRE found Paris as much divided against itself as at the time of his leaving it. 'The only topic of talk there was of Rome, excommunication, Jansenists, Jesuits, a *Unigenitus* Constitution, exiles and imprisonments. An assembly of bishops held at Embrun had just resulted in twenty thousand *lettres de cachet.*' It was then held quite natural to lock up those who differed in opinion from Ministers on matters of religious doctrine, and Saint-Simon himself advised the Regent to have the Jesuits Lallemand, Doucin and Tournemine removed, ' to put the last-named in the keep of Vincennes without paper, ink, or pen, and without talking to any one, but well lodged and fed because of his personal status (he was of good birth) ; the other two in dungeons in different prisons, with dungeon treatment, so that it should not be known where they were, and they might die there.'

As for the men of letters, they excommuni-
cated each other ' because some ingenious
mind had claimed that it was not essential for
tragedy to be in verse.' Voltaire announced
his return by publishing a short piece of writing
entitled *Sottises des Deux Parts*. He showed the
folly of these disputes, recalling the absurd
controversies of the Middle Ages, so completely
forgotten, and foretold that the future would
forget Jesuits and Jansenists alike. ' An aged
doctor said to me : " Sir, in my youth I wrote
against the Formulary and against the Pope ;
I was put in prison and thought myself a
martyr. Nowadays I take no part in anything
and feel myself reasonable." " How do you
occupy yourself ? " I asked him.—" Sir," he
answered me, " I am very fond of money."
Thus do men in their old age smile at the
follies of their youth ; deeds grow old like men
themselves.'

He himself, though young, was fond of
money. He had learned in England that
fortune gives independence. On his return
to France he entered into relations with the
Pâris brothers, the great financiers, who advised him in investing the money he had in-

herited from his father the notary. Part of it he invested in the provision of army supplies, from which, according to his secretary, he made 600,000 *livres*, another part in the Cadiz trade and in vessels trading with America. He succeeded in all. His ships were lucky enough never to be met by corsairs. He even won in the lottery, and before long he had the largest fortune ever amassed by a poet. ' His portfolios were full of contracts, bills of exchange, government stock. It would doubtless have been hard to find in the portfolio of any man of letters so many manuscripts of this kind.'

Neither bastinado nor exile had cured him of his fondness for exalted society. He loved life so much that he wanted to enjoy it in all its forms. A little later, in a poem which he called *Le Mondain*, he depicted the joy of living and the fondness for luxurious delights which were then his dominant sentiments :

> All tastes together reign within my heart ;
> Kindled by every joy, I own each Art.

Science and history, opera and poetry, suppers and sages—he loved everything, he desired everything. Particularly was he enamoured of the stage. England had given him fresh ideas regarding the art of the theatre, and he wished to apply them to the French stage. Not that he was a convert to Shakespeare ; he was too much a Frenchman of his own time to accept Shakespeare as a whole. But amongst the many 'gross flaws' he had caught glimpses of the things of beauty. Whilst yet maintaining the rule of the three unities, could one not write tragedies in France which would have livelier action ? Could not one be so very bold as to show some of these actions on the stage instead of describing them in narrative ? After his return, in 1730, he attempted a tragedy on a political theme. This was *Brutus*. He rehearsed it with his usual ardour, calling out to the actor who played Brutus : ' Good heavens, sir ! Remember that you are Brutus, the strongest of all the Roman consuls, and that you mustn't talk to the god Mars as if you were saying " Holy Mary ! Grant that I draw a hundred-franc ticket in the lottery ! " '

Brutus was a success. Two years later *Zaïre* was a triumph. Like everything that Voltaire did in the theatre, it was a mixture of a spoonful of daring with a heap of caution. In constructing his plot he had remembered Shakespeare's *Othello*, and transposed the subject into a different setting, amongst French knights and kings of Jerusalem. The violent acting of the players, drilled by Voltaire, was something new, and was a partial explanation of the prodigious success. And doubtless, in those scenes that seem to us so chilly, the public could detect the first far trumpets of romanticism.

About the same time Voltaire had published his *History of Charles XII*, which was widely praised. The public were annoyed at his not being in the Academy. If the Ministers and the Court had then decided to leave him alone, he would perhaps have remained all his life only a fashionable playwright.

VII

LETTRES PHILOSOPHIQUES

But by 1731 he had already been forced into
exile again. Adrienne Lecouvreur had died, a
great actress whom Voltaire had greatly admired. The Church refused religious rites of
burial to actors, and Mlle. Lecouvreur had to be
buried in a piece of waste land alongside the
Seine. Voltaire was outraged, followed the
procession, and protested in a spirited poem.
Was he always to see his wavering nation brand
what it most admired ? Must morals and laws
always clash, and how long must the nimble
French mind sleep drugged by superstition ?
Was it only in England that mortal men could
dare to think ?

> Rival of Athens ! London ! Happy land,
> From whence was driv'n the boding, shameful band
> Of prejudice and tyrants. . . .

There no art was contemned, no success un-
rewarded by fame, and Adrienne Lecouvreur

46

In London would have found her honour'd grave
'Mid poets and learnèd, monarchs and the brave.

' This apotheosis of an play-actress was regarded as horrible impiety.' Voltaire took to flight, and lay low in a village in Normandy. Before long there was secretly printed at Rouen a book entitled *Lettres Philosophiques*. It dealt with the English, and was a curious work, as important in its influence as it was slight in its text. It could not be said to be either profound or particularly well informed. But it achieved its author's aim : to make known to Frenchmen those elements in England, almost an unknown land to them, which might make them ponder on the shortcomings of their own institutions and transform their religious or political ideas.

There were first of all five letters on the religious sects : Quakers, Anglicans, Socinians, and Arians. The subject was always a favourite with Voltaire, and it is easy to see why. To show the diversity of religious beliefs is to prove the weakness of each. Furthermore, he was able to make the characters he depicted put forward arguments which he could not have delivered himself without danger. ' My good

D 47

sir,' he says to his Quaker, ' are you baptized ? '
—' No,' answers the Quaker, ' nor my fellow-
believers either.'—' Heavens above ! ' he went
on. ' Then you are not Christians ? '—' Friend,'
answered the Quaker gently, ' do not swear :
we are indeed Christians. But we do not believe that Christianity depends on throwing
water with a pinch of salt on one's head.'—
' But, Lord preserve us ! ' argues Voltaire, outraged by such impiety, ' have you forgotten
that Jesus Christ was baptized by John ? '—
' Friend, keep thy oaths once again,' replies the
benign Quaker. ' Christ did receive baptism
from John, but He never baptized any one, and
we are disciples of Christ, not of John.'—' Ah !
how the Holy Inquisition would burn you ! ' he
exclaims. . . .

Next came two letters on Parliament and
the Government. The power of the Commons
rejoiced the heart of the bourgeois Arouet, as
did also the absence of certain privileges. ' All
this affords the English merchant a just measure
of pride, and he can venture to compare himself, not without reason, to a Roman citizen.
Also, the younger son of a peer of the realm
does not disdain mercantile pursuits. . . .'

There follows what may be called the letters of popularised philosophy, one on the ideas of Locke, which enabled Voltaire to expound his own doctrines for the first time. He believes in God, but will not admit that we can know anything of God beyond his existence and the fact of his having created the world. In the immortality of the soul he believes because it is necessary to the general weal, but finds no trace of that soul in nature, praising Locke for his modest remark that we shall perhaps never be able to know whether a purely material being thinks or not.

Then come some scientific letters on Newton and the laws of attraction, on optics, on the infinite. They all show an inquiring spirit and a quite extensive store of information. And the book ends with letters on tragedy and comedy. There he reveals to the French the poet Shakespeare, ' whom the English regard as a Sophocles. . . . His genius was full of strength and fecundity, of the natural and the sublime, without the smallest spark of fine taste and without the slightest knowledge of the rules.' But although he deplored Shakespeare's ignorance of the rules, he reproached

49

those who had hitherto informed the French only of his errors, and he tried himself to translate into verse one of Shakespeare's finest passages. He chose Hamlet's soliloquy, ' To be or not to be . . .'—and he turned it into a piece of Crébillon. Shakespeare's vigorous wording was replaced by a jargon of abstractions, and the regular swing of the Alexandrines lulled the reader's senses :

> *Demeure ; il faut choisir et passer à l'instant*
> *De la vie à la mort, et de l'être au néant.*
> *Dieux justes ! s'il en est, éclairez mon courage.*
> *Faut-il vieiller courbé sous la main qui m'outrage,*
> *Supporter ou finir mon malheur et mon sort ?*
> *Qui suis-je ? Qui m'arrête ? Et qu'est-ce que la mort ?*
> *C'est la fin de nos maux, c'est mon unique asile ;*
> *Après de longs transports, c'est un sommeil tranquille ;*
> *On s'endort et tout meurt . . .*

But although it was a faithless translation, his comment was shrewd : ' The English poetical genius has, up to the present, resembled a bushy tree of Nature's planting, throwing forth a thousand random boughs and growing strongly but unevenly. If you force its nature and prune it into a tree of the gardens of Marly, it will die.'

No sooner had the book appeared than the

police were prosecuting it. The bookseller was sent to the Bastille. Voltaire had to take refuge in Lorraine, and a decree of the Parlement condemned the *Lettres Philosophiques* to be ' torn and burned in the Palace courtyard, at the foot of the great staircase therein, by the common executioner, as being scandalous, contrary to religion, good morals, and the respect due to the ruling powers '—a decree which was put into force on June 10th, 1734.

It is very much as if to-day, somewhere in America, a book were burned by the hangman containing explanations of the theories of Einstein, the Soviet constitution, and the plays of Pirandello.

VIII

THE DIVINE EMILIE

MADAME DU CHÂTELET is a remarkable instance of the immortality which illicit love will ensure for a woman, provided that its object be illustrious. She was a Mlle. de Breteuil, and like many girls of the period was highly educated. She knew Latin and was fond of the sciences. She had studied mathematics, and translated the *Principia* of Newton, adding an algebraic commentary. Add to this the fact that she was, as Voltaire said, ' something of a philosopher and a shepherdess,' and that she wrote a treatise on *Happiness*. All these labours would to-day be in sorry oblivion had she not been the mistress of Voltaire.

When he met her she was twenty-seven, and he was thirty-nine. He was still bubbling over with his journeying in England, and could only talk of ' Mr. Loke ' and ' Sir Newton.' That was exactly what interested the Marquise du Châtelet, along with love, which her husband hardly practised. She was intellectual and sensuous — an agreeable blend. She liked books, diamonds, algebra, petticoats, and physics. In this she was like Voltaire, who was curious about everything and insatiable in activity. Women called her plain. Mme. du Deffand has sketched a famous and malicious portrait of her : ' Tall, sapless, narrow-hipped and narrow-breasted, heavy arms, heavy legs, enormous feet. . . .' And Mme. de Créqui : ' My cousin Emilie was a colossus in all her proportions, a marvel of strength and a prodigy of clumsiness. She had a skin like a nutmeg-grater.' But can women be trusted when faced with a woman who is intelligent, amorous, admired, and has conquered the most famous man of the age ?

She entered Voltaire's life at a moment when he needed a safe haven. Persecution is a habit. The law and the Ministers had got into the habit of persecuting this poet. Vintimille, the Archbishop of Paris, ' who loved women passionately and philosophers not at all,' complained to the lieutenant of police about a certain epistle to *Uranie*. There was talk, too, about an epic on the Maid of Orleans, an ill-kept secret which was causing terrible scandal. The Keeper of the Seals summoned the author and threatened that if the poem appeared he would have him ' buried in a dungeon.' It is vexing to have an apostolic vocation without having the martyr's. Voltaire wished to think freely, but not to live in the Bastille. Mme. du Châtelet offered him hiding in the château of Cirey, a property of hers in the border country very close to Lorraine, whither it would be easy to flee in the event of further proceedings against him. He accepted, and spent the next fourteen years in close intimacy with her.

A long liaison, and not without storms. What with Voltaire's excitability and the fiery temperament of Mme. du Châtelet, sparks were often flying. On these occasions they would both become frenzied, shouting, and falling back on English in order to insult each other in front of their guests. But active people are free from rancour. There was a laboratory at Cirey, a gallery of chemistry, entirely constructed by M. du Châtelet at Voltaire's expense, whither Voltaire and Mme. du Châtelet repaired daily to carry out experiments or to write. Unbeknown to each other, they were both competing for a prize of the Academy of Sciences for a study of the nature of fire ; such warmth did Mme. du Châtelet put into the composition of her paper that, to calm herself, she had to plunge her stout arms for hours in cold water. Voltaire was composing a study of the philosophy of Newton. Mathematicians, such as Clairault and Maupertuis, came to visit these two amateur colleagues. The Président Hénault, stopping at Cirey, found a monk installed there, a skilled geometer. He admired the plain and elegant building, the rooms filled with apparatus, the laborious mode of life.

Visitors came also from the little neighbouring court of Lunéville. A certain Mme. de Graffigny came for refuge to Cirey, after some domestic upset, and was welcomed there by 'the nymph of the place,' the divine Emilie, and by the ' idol,' Voltaire himself, a little candlestick in his hand. With them was living ' the big cat,' or Mme. de Champbonin, and sometimes, but rarely, ' the goodman,' that is to say, the Marquis du Châtelet, a discreet gentleman with no taste for mathematics. Life was wonderfully full. Mme. du Châtelet and the

Idol only appeared at supper, which was taken in the physics gallery, facing the globes and instruments. Conversation ran upon poetry, science, and art ; it was always kept on a light key, except when Voltaire's enemies were mentioned (Jean-Baptiste Rousseau or Desfontaines). Then he would break all bounds, bursting into invective, maledictions, and excommunications. Apart from this weakness he was charming, offering his guests now a tragedy or an epistle, now the beginning of his history of Louis XIV., now a scientific paper or a few pages on the Chinese or the Arabs.

For he was interested in all things : ' I could wish that Newton had written operettas,' he wrote, ' I should esteem him all the higher. . . . One must give one's soul every possible form ; it is a flame that God has entrusted to us, and we must feed it with whatever we find most precious. We should let all imaginable modes of being enter into us, open all the doorways of our minds to all the sciences and all the sentiments. Provided that they do not enter pell-mell, there is room for all.' And further : ' I admit that I should be very glad to have once in my life courted the muse of opera with success. I love all the Nine, and one should have all the lovely favours that one can, but without being too much of a gallant.'

In the letters of Mme. de Graffigny one catches glimpses of the intimate life of this pair of strange lovers : ' Madame is tyrannical, and Voltaire rebellious. If he appears in one coat she orders him to change it. He makes the excuse that he will be cold. She insists. Voices grow higher. Voltaire goes out, sends word that he has the colic, and that's the end of the pleasures. The sulky twain reappear, with fond words of English for each other. Voltaire sits down at table again, bidding the footmen take good care of Madame. Then, after dinner, if he is in good humour, he works the magic-lantern himself. He is excellent thereat, intro-ducing the Abbé Desfontaines, the Jesuits, Rousseau. His animation increases when he knocks over the spirit-lamp. He burns his fingers. He feels upset, revives, and proposes a puppet-show, or a comedy or a tragedy. He deals out a score of manuscripts, which one is obliged to read at sight. He insists on the others taking parts. One has to curl one's hair, get excited, go over pieces again.' Mme. de Graffigny relates that within twenty-four hours the guests at Cirey rehearsed and performed thirty-three acts from various pieces ! ' Alas ! how short is time ! '

IX

LOUIS XIV AND FREDERICK THE GREAT

In the solitude of Cirey Voltaire had written
much and explored wide fields of research. The
part of his labours which won him most fame
amongst his contemporaries is not the best
part. It includes verse *Discourses on Man*, in-
ferior to Pope's, some *Epistles*, which are often
pleasing but never admirable (the most charming are those which he threw carelessly into his
letters), and tragedies, *Alzire* and *Mahomet*,
topical dramas, philosophical and sententious,
' the underlying meanings of which make up
their value.' To the men of 1740 this poet
was the real Voltaire. As soon as he talked of
science, as in his writings on Newton, the
savants protested. As soon as he published a
history, ' the historians,' said Condorcet, ' accused his work of being a mere romance,
because it had all the interest of a romance.'
The poor man did not know how to be dull.
How could he be taken seriously ?

All his life long he was curious regarding history ; and if we bear in mind what history was like before him, we must admit that he brought it a comparative measure of exactness. Those were the days when Father Daniel, confronted by eleven or twelve hundred volumes of original papers and manuscripts in the Royal Library, spent an hour in skimming them and declared himself content with his researches. Voltaire had more precision ; he looked at the documents, sought out originals, questioned witnesses. To him, history did not consist only of relating the lives and exploits of monarchs, but showing the transformations of peoples, the advance of morality, literature, and the arts. ' Not *history*, but *his stories*,' was his comment on the Abbé de Fleury's work. During his stay at Cirey, if he did not complete his *Essay on Morals*, he at least prepared and composed a great part of that universal history, and also his *Century of Louis XIV*, which was to be the crown of that history. Later on, when he had become Historiographer Royal, he added a *Louis XV*.

Much that is good and much that is bad can be said of the *Essay on Morals*. Voltaire must be admired for having been one of the first to give appropriate place to the Arabian and Chinese civilisations, and for the then proscribed study of comparative religion. But the book is pitted with errors, some inevitable because the truth (or at any rate *our* truth) was unknown, others less pardonable. Montesquieu said that Voltaire wrote history to glorify his own monastery as much as any Benedictine did ; and that is true. In the *Essay on Morals* he preaches his religion of anti-religion on every page. Everywhere we find his obsessing ideas : (*a*) to show that Bossuet was wrong in explaining universal history by the designs of Providence (to Voltaire it was explained, not by ultimate causes, but by the blind action of small efficacious causes) ; (*b*) to show that the history of mankind has been a more or less insane sequence of crimes, follies, and disasters, but that men are approaching an age wherein Reason will put order into everything ; and (*c*) to eliminate the supernatural. And in that last, Voltaire's criterion does not seem sound : to him anything that is not really likely is false, but the pity is that the zone of likelihood has no very definite boundaries.

Voltaire's great weakness as a historian is that, being an intellectualist philosopher, he does not understand the sentimental and mystical cravings of other men. He does not perceive that underneath the multiplicity of sects and rites there is always the common ground of a need for rites. This disability is all the more curious because Voltaire analyses so admirably the nature of man's common heritage as regards the family, or love, or friendship. ' Voltaire fully realised that the King was not the nation, that a congress of diplomatists did not inform us about the habits of the shopkeeper or the revolts of a peasantry, but he failed to appreciate that a shopkeeper in Baghdad was not a shopkeeper of the Marais, and that a peasant in Crusading days did not rebel for the same reasons as a tiller of the soil under Louis xv.' None of these weaknesses is to be found in the *Century of Louis XIV*. There he was concerned with a time he knew well and whose actors he had himself seen. There he shows himself as the first of the great modern historians.

*   *   *

As a consolation for the hostility of the French Court, Voltaire was able during his sojourn at Cirey, to sample one royal friendship—that of Frederick of Prussia.

Frederick had been reared by French refugees. His greatest longing was to shine as a great poet and prose-writer in the French tongue. It was no foolish desire, for he wrote the language well and did not lack wit. Nevertheless he was well aware that he was not free from faults, and that these spoiled his verses. It was natural that he should feel an idolatrous admiration for a man who seemed to excel in all branches of letters, who was at once the best epic poet, the best tragic poet, the best letter-writer, and the best historian of his time.

One day in 1736 Voltaire received a letter: 'Sir—Although I have not the satisfaction of being acquainted with you personally, you are none the less familiar to me through your works. They are treasuries of the mind. . . .' A correspondence was begun, in a highly affectionate tone. 'Do not suppose,' wrote the young Frederick, 'that I push my scepticism to extremities : I believe, for instance, that there is only one God, and only one Voltaire in the world.' Voltaire replied that the French verses of this heir to a German crown were ' very pretty, very well written, and in the best tone in the world.' ' Epithets cost us nothing,' he remarked in later years about this correspondence.

In 1740 Frederick became King. The philosophers were deeply moved by the thought of there being an ' enlightened ' prince on one of the thrones of Europe, who would put their precepts into practice and who was the friend of Voltaire. The new King would gladly have enticed his master and poet to his Court, but there was one serious obstacle — Mme. du Châtelet. She would not have allowed Voltaire to leave ; and as for bringing her to Potsdam, that was out of the question—Frederick only cared for grenadiers of his own sex.

Nevertheless, he wished to set eyes on Voltaire, and he arranged a first meeting in Belgium. Voltaire was surprised at finding a young King in uniform, on a camp bed. Europe was soon shown that the man who had written an *Anti-Machiavelli* before his coronation, would be the most machiavellian and warlike of all the kings in Europe. In 1741 he invaded

Austria, at that time France's hereditary enemy. The French applauded Frederick's success, the more so because he had his triumph celebrated by France's own men of letters. Voltaire was at Lille, where he was producing the *Mahomet* which he dared not stage in Paris, when news came of the King of Prussia's victory at Molwitz. He was seen to rise in his box, papers in his hand, asking silence of the public, and he announced that he had just had news of his victory from His Majesty the King of Prussia. His Majesty had sent the tidings in French, and in toy verselets :

> From a flimsy framework town
> Which Boreas would fain hurl down,
> Where we presently do dwell,
> Edifice like cockle-shell . . .

and so on. This meant : ' I am writing from under canvas.' The Lille public responded to the reading with great acclamations.

For a moment Voltaire fancied he would be able to use this royal friendship to become the diplomat and man of action he would so gladly have been. In 1743 the French Court was anxious to know whether, in a conflict with Austria and England, it could count on the support of Frederick II., and one Minister was inspired to make use of Voltaire. He was despatched on a secret mission to Potsdam. To throw Frederick off the scent he made a pretence of asking sanctuary of him, declaring that he was pursued by the Bishop of Mirepoix, against whom he had written a satire.

But Frederick was much too astute to fall into such a trap. He gave Voltaire a warm welcome, introduced him to the princesses for whom he had written madrigals, entertained him with flute recitals, and wheedling him, sent his guest's letters to the Bishop of Mirepoix whom they attacked. He expected a double outcome from this treachery : either the Bishop would lose his temper and force the Court to act, whereupon Voltaire, exiled once again, would be forced to remain in Prussia and the King would gain a secretary of genius to correct his epigrams ; or, on the other hand, the Bishop would not react, which would be proof of collusion and of Voltaire's deceit.

The second hypothesis was sound, and was made quite obvious. And so, when Voltaire presented Frederick with a memorandum and a request to write his replies to it in the

margin, he received back his paper covered
with verses. He asked whether the King could
be counted upon against England. But Frederick answered :

> What is it you would have me at ?
> The climax ? God from the Machine ?
> But peer more closely at my mien—
> I'm not so mischievous as that !

And all that the poet-ambassador brought
back from his embassy was King Frederick's
rhyming.

X

FAVOURS AND MISHAPS

ABOUT his fiftieth year Voltaire, hitherto
treated by the Court as a dangerous opponent
and a man hardly to be tolerated, became suddenly a courtier and a favourite. The reasons
for his change of fortune were many : the
German negotiations, in which he had appeared an important, if not an efficacious,
figure ; the rise to power of M. d'Argenson, a
philosopher-Minister, who had been his fellow-
pupil at Louis-le-Grand and, being an honest
man, was called ' d'Argenson the Stupid ' by
the courtiers ; the advent, as Louis xv.'s mistress, of Mme. Le Normant d'Etioles (later the
Marquise de Pompadour), whom Voltaire had
known very well and whose confidant he had
been ; and finally, Voltaire's own desires. In
the life of nearly all men there comes a critical
time when they fear some lessening of their
powers. They then feel anxious to consolidate

their gains and to lean thenceforth on the crutches of honours. These are flimsy supports.

With *Mérope*, Voltaire had just enjoyed a prodigious success in the theatre. The whole public, upstanding to acclaim him, had cried out to the youthful Mme. de Villars : 'Mme. de Villars—embrace Voltaire !' This popular renown was not enough for him ; he wanted titles —and he had them. He was appointed Gentleman-in-ordinary and Historiographer Royal. The archives were put at his disposal to write a history of the campaigns of Louis xv. He took a fancy to this vocation of official historian.

At the time of Cardinal Fleury's death, he had tried unsuccessfully to enter the French Academy. His failure had been arranged by the ' right-thinkers,' but he set about placating them. He wrote a letter to Father La Tour, declaring his respect for religion and his attachment to the Jesuits. ' Notwithstanding the skill with which he handled his phrases in this letter,' says Condorcet, ' it would surely have been better to renounce the Academy than to stoop to writing it. In the end Mme. de Pompadour had him entrusted with the composition of a *divertissement* for the marriage of the Infanta, and the Academy was the reward for this work.

> My *Henri* and my sad *Zaïre*,
> My fair American, *Alzire*,
> Brought me not once a Kingly glance :
> Foes and not Fame were all my chance.
> But now I'm heap'd with wealth and crowns
> For writing farces fit for clowns.

The pious still held his *Mahomet* against him. Dexterously he sent his tragedy to Pope Benedict XIV., ' an enlightened and reasonable Pontiff,' who replied that *Mahomet* was a ' *bellissima tragedia*' which he had read ' *cum summo piacere*,' and sent him indulgences and the ' *apostolica benedizione*.' After which there was nothing left for the Academy but to elect him, which they did.

But place, as always happens to those who seek it, did not bring happiness to Voltaire. The favour of kings is transitory, but never so their disfavour, and Louis XV. never liked Voltaire. The King was too quick-witted not to fear the quick wits of others, and the philosophers in his eyes were foes to the Crown at a time when they were revered by many of his courtiers. Towards the end of the performance of the *Temple de la Gloire* at Versailles, the piece in which the poet had sought to portray the King under the guise of the Emperor Trajan, Voltaire moved over from his place near the royal box, and said in audible tones: 'Is Trajan satisfied?' Louis xv. turned towards him, stared at him fixedly, and said nothing. Such familiarities were not to his taste.

There were more serious incidents. One day when Voltaire and Mme. du Châtelet were playing cards together with the Queen, Madame lost heavily. Voltaire whispered in English that she was playing with rogues, and that she ought to leave the tables at once. An argument, very offensive to those present, broke out between the elderly lovers, who were persuaded, as French people always are, that one need only speak in a foreign language to be understood by nobody. But in a few moments they detected, from the stirring of the company and the remarks they caught, that they were both heard and understood. Terror seized them at once. Voltaire had visions of the Bastille. Mme. du Châtelet saw herself robbed of her Idol. During the night they ordered their

carriage and fled to Sceaux, to the Duchesse
du Maine.

This 'opposition Court' was a natural refuge.
The Duc du Maine, natural son of Louis XIV.
and Mme. de Montespan, had married a grand-
daughter of the great Condé, a young woman
who, though almost a dwarf, was ' curious,
bold, imperious, and fantastical.' She cherished
dreams of supreme power for her timid husband, and the couple had formed high hopes
at the moment of the death of Louis XIV., who
had, in point of fact, desired to favour the Duc
du Maine by his will. But the hatred of the
Court had shouldered them away from power.

The Duchesse had found consolation in form-
ing her own small Court of philosophers and
wits in her valley of Sceaux. She was culti-
vated, spoke well, and bandied gallant verses
with those whom she styled her ' shepherds of
Sceaux.' With them she provided herself with
an illusion of power. This was the Court in
which, all unexpectedly, Voltaire and Mme.
du Châtelet ensconced themselves. Mme. de
Staal-Delaunay has described their arrival :
' They appeared at midnight, like a pair of
ghosts, with an odour of embalmment which

they seemed to have brought from their tomb. Supper was just ending. Still, they were famished ghosts. They had to have supper, and, what's more, beds—which were not ready.'

As guests they were exacting. They were never seen until ten o'clock at night, for they spent the daytime, one, in writing a chapter of history, the other, in commenting on Newton. Mme. du Châtelet could not stand the slightest noise, and she had for ever to be changing her rooms. 'She is now passing her principles in review. This exercise she repeats every year; without it they might escape, and perhaps bolt so far that she would never catch one of them again.'

Dread of the Bastille made Voltaire live in a small out-of-the-way apartment from which he only came down at night, to sup with the Duchesse du Maine at her bedside. 'The Princess greatly enjoyed seeing and conversing with him. The liveliness of his talk diverted her, and she proved instructive to him by her numerous old anecdotes of the Court which were new to him. Sometimes, after the collation, he read a tale or a short novel which he had written during the day expressly for her

73

diversion.' In this way there came into being *La Vision de Babouc, Memnon, Scarmentado, Micromégas, Zadig*, a few chapters of which he wrote daily.

These miniature philosophic novels, always composed to prove some moral truth, were written in a deliciously light-hearted style. So much did the Duchesse du Maine like them that other people became desirous of knowing them, and Voltaire was pressed into reading them aloud. He read like a great actor. The tales had a vast success and his listeners implored him to print them. For a long time he refused, saying that these little drawing-room trifles did not deserve the light of day.

A fresh alarm induced him to return to his haven at Cirey. It was winter. The axle of the carriage ' broke in the middle of the night, right out in the country. The coach upset. Whilst it was being repaired, Voltaire and Mme. du Châtelet contemplated the moon and the stars, discussing astronomy.' The boy put icicles into the holy-water. The man, seated in the snow with his mistress, gazed contentedly at the lifeless stars. With such ingenious symbolism did the gods pattern the life and loves of Voltaire !

XI

SAINT-LAMBERT

CIREY was not very far from a miniature capital.
In Lunéville, Stanislas Leczinski, former King
of Poland and father of the Queen of France,
reigned over Lorraine. His dwindled Court
consisted chiefly of a mistress and a confessor.
Menou, the Jesuit confessor, hated the mistress,
Mme. de Boufflers, and about 1749 conceived
the notion of replacing her by Mme. du Châtelet. It was no secret in the country that the
latter's old-standing liaison with Voltaire had
become, through his maladies, almost platonic.
But the lady retained her fiery temperament,
and for all her anxiety to keep her great man,
she apparently did not revolt against the idea
of pleasure.

Voltaire and Mme. du Châtelet were invited
to stay at the Court of Lorraine, 'where they
diverted the good King Stanislas with concerts,
fêtes, and spectacles.' Mme. du Châtelet played

in comedy and tragedy, sang, conquered Mme.
de Boufflers, whose ally instead of rival she
became, and conquered also M. de Saint-
Lambert, a captain in the regiment of Prince
de Beauvau, a handsome, cold, witty young
man who was equally adept in verse-making
and love-making.

One evening, after a whole day's work on the
history of Louis xv., Voltaire entered Mme. du
Châtelet's room without being announced, and
there found his mistress and Saint-Lambert on
a sofa, 'conversing together on matters that
were neither poetry nor philosophy.' He was
furiously insulting, went out, and ordered his
horses : he would leave Lunéville that very
night. Mme. du Châtelet forbade the lackeys
to order the horses, and went up to Voltaire's
room to pacify him. 'What!' he cried.
'You want me to believe you after what I
saw ?'—'No,' she said. 'I still love you, but
for some time you have complained that you
were not so strong as you were, and that you
couldn't go on. . . . It is a great grief to me.
I am very far from desiring your demise ; your
health is very dear to me. You, on your side,
have always shown great care for mine. Since

you agree that you could no longer take care of it, save to your own detriment, how can you be angry that one of your friends is coming to your aid?'—'Ah, Madame,' he said. 'As always, you are right. But if things must be so, pray, at least, see that they don't go on before my eyes.'

Next day Saint-Lambert himself came to see Voltaire and apologised. 'My boy,' said Voltaire, 'I have forgotten everything, and it is I who am wrong. You are in the happy age when a man loves and takes pleasure. Enjoy those moments—they are too brief.' Some time later he wrote a comedy on the episode, which he did not deem fitting to publish.

The old couple came back to Cirey reconciled, and were on the point of returning to Paris when Mme. du Châtelet, usually so lively, became anxious. At the age of forty-four, she was pregnant. It was only natural that she should take Voltaire into her confidence. He advised that Saint-Lambert should immediately be summoned, and a council of three was held as to the means of having the child acknowledged by the Marquis du Châtelet. Everything was arranged like a comedy. Summoned on the pretext of arranging certain family business, M. du Châtelet came to the château and was welcomed with every token of affection. Voltaire and Saint-Lambert were both there ; the people of the neighbourhood were invited ; a little fête was given ; there was a supper. M. du Châtelet was given plenty to eat and drink, and recounted his campaigns. His stories were attentively listened to. He was duly flattered. Mme. du Châtelet had made a most alluring toilette. Her husband became gallant and took on the airs of youth. In the end, after three weeks of bewitchments, his lady avowed to him that certain signs pointed to her being enceinte. He fell on her neck, embraced her, and proudly told the news to everybody. She was saved.

Her time of waiting was spent in sojourns in Paris and at Cirey. She strove hard to seem cheerful, but she had melancholy forebodings. She thought she would die in childbed. The birth, however, passed off well. When she felt the first pangs, she scribbled some remarks on Newton. In a letter Voltaire remarked : ' Whilst scribbling her Newton this evening Mme. du Châtelet felt uncomfortable. She called her maid, who had just time to stretch out her apron and receive a little girl, who was carried to her cradle.'

But things went wrong, and on the sixth day she died. M. du Châtelet, Voltaire, and Saint-Lambert were present, all three lamenting. Voltaire, in the extremity of his grief, went out of doors, slipped, and fell. Saint-Lambert had followed him and picked him up. On recovering his senses, he said : ' Oh, my young friend, it was *you* who killed her for me ! ' For a long time his despair continued. He wandered about the great château where everything reminded him of Emilie. He remembered their arrival, the bales of tapestry which she had so energetically unpacked, and the skill with which she had converted the bleak and desolate place into a temple of love, friendship, and science.

At last he returned to Paris. To begin with, nobody could talk with him. For quite a long time his friends had seen his weariness of this woman, and they were amazed at the bitterness of his grief. Marmontel describes finding him in tears : ' he had often told me that she was like a fury clamped to his steps, but I let him weep and I mourned with him

F 79

myself. But so as to point out that in the very cause of her death there might be some ground for solace, I asked him what she had died of? "What she died of? Don't you know? My dear friend, he killed her, the brute ! He gave her a child." And once again he started on his eulogies of this incomparable woman, re-doubling his tears and sobs. Just then Chau-velin arrived on the scene, and told some amusing anecdote—I have forgotten what. And Voltaire burst into laughter with him.' For, like many great men, he was childishly mercurial.

It was through the theatre that his zest for life was at last restored.

XII

THE KING OF PRUSSIA

For a long time Frederick the Great had been eager to attach Voltaire to his Court. With Mme. du Châtelet dead, his invitations became pressing, and Voltaire was not indifferent to them. The King of France refused to admit him to his supper-parties; the King of Prussia wrote to him in verse. The display of Court favour towards his rival, Crébillon, crowned his despite, and the only obstacle outstanding was the avarice of Frederick. He was quite willing to pay Voltaire an allowance, but not his travelling expenses. Furthermore, since the death of his mistress, Voltaire had set up house with a niece, Mme. Denis. He wished to bring her. That meant a thousand *livres* more, and Frederick would not have spent a penny on bringing a woman to his Court.

Pride won where money failed. Voltaire was told that a mischievous French poet, d'Arnaud

Baculard, had been attached to Frederick's Court, and that the King had written him an epistle such as he might have penned for Voltaire himself. It contained, they said, these sacrilegious lines :

> The French Apollo sinks in slow decline :
> Come hither, Arnaud, rise thyself, and shine !

Instantly Voltaire wrote back a rhyming letter to the King : so, Frederick had been flattering the stripling Arnaud . . . in those light verses of his which were current in France . . . sixty winters, nearly, had whitened Voltaire's head, whilst Frederick's were crowned with all manner of laurels—

> Can it, great Frederick, be fair
> To spoil me of my poor white hair ?

And having finished writing the verses, he leapt out of bed, crying : ' Voltaire setting and Baculard rising ? And the King writes this monstrous foolishness ? ' dancing up and down with rage. In his nightshirt he apostrophised the King of Prussia : ' I'll go ! ' he kept saying, ' I'll go and teach him to understand which men are which ! ' The journey was decided upon.

He had to ask authorisation of the Court to set off. Explaining his business to the competent Minister, he asked whether they would not like to charge him with some mission in Berlin. 'None,' answered the Minister ; the King turned his back, and the Dauphin likewise. Voltaire had got Frederick II. to write to Louis xv., asking sanction to keep Voltaire permanently ; grumblingly the King replied that he would be delighted, remarking to his courtiers that it would be one fool the more at the Prussian Court and one fool the less at his own.

'Beginnings are always agreeable.' Voltaire's beginning at Potsdam was magnificent. He was welcomed at his carriage door by the King in person. Fêtes were staged for the performance of his tragedies, which he witnessed in the midst of the royal family. As he passed by, a whole people whispered : 'Voltaire . . . Voltaire. . . .' He had the Cross of Merit on his breast, the chamberlain's key on his back, and 28,000 *livres* as an allowance. The small circle of the King's intimates, savants and men of letters, began to find this new favourite a decided encumbrance. They included a few Frenchmen, amongst them La Mettrie, of whom Voltaire remarked that he was the 'atheist in ordinary,' Deprades, who had maintained before the Sorbonne itself that Moses was the boldest of historians, the famous d'Arnaud Baculard, whose star was rising only to be immediately extinguished by Voltaire, who had him sent packing by the King, and above all, the learned Maupertuis, whom Frederick had made president of his Academy of Sciences. He was a good mathematician, chiefly renowned for having computed the degrees of the meridian in the Polar region in Lapland, and having brought home two Lapps who had delighted the Parisian salons for a week or so. When Voltaire arrived Maupertuis happened to be away ; the mathematician returned to find him installed at Court, a key on his back and plastered with ribands, a man of letters who had committed two crimes against his self-respect. He promised himself to put an end to this scandal. Voltaire's two crimes were these : first, that in his discourse to the French Academy he had made a list of great living men, omitting Maupertuis ; second, that Voltaire was his compatriot, and more renowned than himself.

Nothing is more dangerous than small groups. Talk goes the rounds, swirling like water in an eddy. The Potsdam circle showed its formidable side. Frederick, as d'Argens said, was a coquette who, in order to keep several lovers, made none of them happy. The circle passed round the story that Voltaire, on receiving one of the King's manuscripts for correction, had murmured : ' The King sends me his dirty linen to launder.' At the same time they brought back word to Voltaire that His Majesty had remarked : ' I shall need him for a year still : one squeezes the orange and flings the rind away.' Whereupon Voltaire compared himself to Plato at the Court of the tyrant Dionysius. ' But Plato,' he added, ' didn't waste his time correcting bad verse.' This remark in its turn was passed on, with commentary.

The relationship of the King and his guest was becoming curdled. Voltaire was fond of business transactions, and could not resist certain speculations in Prussia, which happened to be legally somewhat shady. He had done so through the agency of a Jew, named Herschel or Hirschel. Each accused the other of being a swindler. Herschel was put in prison, but Voltaire's enemies upheld him and Frederick was roused to a show of bad temper : ' You have made a dreadful hubbub in town. I have managed for my own part to keep peace in my house until your arrival here, and I warn you that if you have a passion for intrigue and cabals, you have certainly come to the wrong place.' If Voltaire had imagined that in Prussia he would find a King less stern than the King of France, this dry tone must have given him food for thought.

Another affair brought the quarrel with the Potsdam circle to a head. Maupertuis had published a treatise on what he termed ' the law of least effort,' in which he maintained that nature, in the distribution of forces, always uses the minimum. He was extremely proud of his ' minimum,' and was for ever explaining everything thereby. Another member of the Berlin Academy, Koenig, was induced to say that this law could already be found in Leibniz, although that philosopher had rejected it. Maupertuis denied Leibniz's letter and accused Koenig of forgery, although he was a genuine scientist and a respected figure.

Berlin was united in its resentment of the accusation, but dared not tell the King, who shielded Maupertuis. But the latter had just published a piece of writing which left a flank opening to ridicule, and Voltaire, the irrepressible Voltaire, could not resist the double temptation to right an injustice and air his wit. He published the *Diatribe du Docteur Akakia*, in which he made fun of certain of Maupertuis's ideas, such as that of smearing all invalids with resin to check the danger of perspiration. The jest was held to be lacking in respect to the King. The pamphlet was confiscated and burnt by the public hangman. The ways of philosopher-kings were devilish like those of tyrant kings.

Voltaire sent back his chamberlain's key and his Cross to the King, with these verses :

> Here I restore, with heart sore grieved,
> That which most fondly I received :
> So doth the portrait of the faithless fair
> Come from her lover in his soured despair.

Frederick restored both key and riband, but requested him to leave. His departure from Germany proved difficult. At Frankfurt he was arrested by an insolent official who claimed

the return of ' the poeshies ' of the King his
master. Frederick's 'poeshies,' as it happened,
were packed with the baggage, left behind at
Leipzig. Voltaire was clapped in gaol at
Frankfurt, and Mme. Denis too, who had come
to meet him. It was all very tiresome.

XIII

THE PHILOSOPHER'S DENS

AFTER the Frankfurt adventure Voltaire knew beyond any peradventure that he could taste liberty no more in Germany than in France. To return to Paris was impossible ; the King of France never wished to see him there again. That was a mistake on the King's part, for, as it has rightly been said, Voltaire's exile marked the divorce between the Court and the men of letters. Louis XIV. had welcomed them and kept them on the leash ; by despising them, Louis XV. unleashed them. Writers are the builders of that public opinion which no government, even absolute, can dispense with. Voltaire in flight spelled doom to the monarchy.

He passed by way of Colmar and took refuge for a few weeks at the Abbey of Senones, where the Benedictines' library somewhat paradoxically helped him in his progress with the *Essay on Morals*. The old monk of anti-clericalism lived appreciatively in the refectory of the scholarly clerks, and had ' a horrible rubbish-heap of erudition ' compiled by the Benedictines. It was, he said, quite a pretty trick, to enter the enemies' camp to obtain arms against them. He then took the waters at Plombières, where he found his d'Argental friends and his two nieces, Mme. Denis and Mme. de Fontaine. Passing through Lyons, where he was enthusiastically welcomed, he at last headed for Switzerland. In that republican land, he thought, he would be shielded from royal princes, imagining rather ingenuously that, having themselves been persecuted, the Reformers must be incapable of persecuting. He arrived in Geneva on December 12th, 1754. He was now sixty.

He supped with Dr. Tronchin, a noted physician, and then obtained the loan for a few weeks of the château of Prangins, meanwhile looking for a house of his own. He first rented one half-way between Lausanne and the Lake, but it was a house for summer use and Mme. Denis was chilled to the bone. They then looked in Geneva itself, and found a large property called Sur-Saint-Jean, which Voltaire renamed Les Délices, to escape such saintly tutelage. There was a hitch because no Catholic could own property in Geneva ; but it was overcome by having the house bought by Tronchin with money borrowed from Voltaire, who had a life tenancy paid for in the guise of interest. For a long time back he had been investing part of his fortune in life annuities, securing favourable terms by reason of his thinness and pallor.

He immediately began signing his letters ' Voltaire the Swiss,' describing the delights of the view from his house ; and avid as ever for activity, he began building, decorating, and planting. ' Mme. Denis and I are busy building dwellings for our guests and hens. We have coaches built, and wheelbarrows. We plant orange trees and tulip bulbs, roses and carrots. We lack everything. Carthage must be founded.'

Hitherto Voltaire had lived under other people's roofs and amassed a great fortune. His desire now was to live the life of a great landlord. He had four carriages, postillions, and lackeys ; he kept open table. Naturally he built himself a theatre, and when the actor

Lekain came to see him he arranged a performance of *Zaïre*. These performances were attended by all the great Genevese families. Before long the pastors began to see dangers in these diversions, sermons were preached against Voltaire in the churches of Geneva, and then he could only use his theatre by stealth.

This was the beginning of his revulsion. The clamour raised by an article he wrote for the *Encyclopaedia* on Geneva increased his anxiety. In this he had praised the Protestant ministers for believing neither in the Bible nor in Hell, and in being like himself simple Deists. Such eulogy was not to their taste. Furthermore, he had written that Calvin had ' cruelty in his soul ' ; and that gave offence. In vain did he write to his printer, protesting that his manuscript had been misread, and that he had written ' austerity,' not ' cruelty.' The game of denials was familiar to him, but all this hubbub showed that, after all, Geneva was no more philosophical than Paris. ' I have a great liking for free peoples,' he said, ' but I much prefer being master in my own house.'

As complete tranquillity was impossible

either in France or in Switzerland, the safest thing was to have one foot in each country, and even, as Voltaire said, four feet. With two châteaux on the shore of the Lake and two along the frontier, he could at the slightest alarm take flight, start arguing, and wait for the storm to blow over. It happened that just then two estates were for sale in French territory near Geneva, the *comté* of Tournay, with all seignorial rights, and the château of Ferney. Purchasing both, he established himself in an inexpugnable position. 'I lean my left flank on the Jura, my right on the Alps, and I have the Lake of Geneva in front of my camp. A handsome château on the confines of France, the hermitage of Les Délices on Genevan territory, a fine house at Lausanne : in this way I creep from den to den, escaping from Kings and from armies.'

XIV

LIFE AT FERNEY

IN the eyes of posterity, nearly every great man is stabilised at one age of life. The Byron of legend is the handsome youth of 1812, and not the full-grown man, prematurely ageing, with thinning hair, whom Lady Blessington knew. Tolstoy is the shaggy old peasant with a broad girdle circling his rustic blouse. The Voltaire of legend is the thin, mischievous old man of Ferney, as Houdon carved him, sneering, his skeleton form bent under its white marble dressing-gown, but bent as a spring is bent, ready to leap. For twenty years Voltaire, at Ferney, was a dying man : he had been one all his life. ' In his health, about which he was for ever complaining, in that Voltairean constitution, robust enough to withstand the most extreme mental activity and frail enough to make any other excess difficult to sustain, he had a valuable prop which he used to wonderful advantage.' [1]

[1] Sainte-Beuve.

His Ferney retreat was populous. Voltaire
said that sages retire into solitude and become
sapless with ennui. At Ferney he knew neither
ennui nor solitude. His circle there included,
first, his two nieces: Mme. Denis was 'a round,
plump little woman of about fifty, a rather impossible woman, plain and good-natured, an
unintentional and harmless liar ; devoid of wit
and with no semblance of having any ; shouting, deciding things, talking politics, versifying,
talking reason, talking nonsense ; in everything
quite unpretentious and certainly shocking
nobody.' [1] Voltaire had purchased Ferney in
her name, conditionally on her signing a private
reservation for his usufruct ; but on com-
pletion of the purchase she refused to sign
this document, not to expel her uncle, but
to hold him in her power, a circumstance
which was the root of a great quarrel. Mme.
de Fontaine, the other niece, was more appeal-
ing and manageable ; she was particularly
fond of painting, and filled the house with
beautiful nudes after Natoire and Boucher,
' to quicken her uncle's ageing blood.' He
relished these. ' One should have some copying

[1] Mme. de Graffigny.

done at the Palais Royal,' he wrote to her, ' of whatever is most beautiful and most immodest there.'

The two nieces came and went ; the permanent guests were a secretary, the faithful Wagnière, and a Jesuit, Father Adam. It may seem surprising to find a Jesuit in Voltaire's old age, but in his heart of hearts he retained a certain fondness for the Reverend Fathers ' who had reared him nicely enough.' Father Adam was a great chess player and had a daily game with Voltaire. ' This good Father,' said the latter, ' may not be one of the world's great men, but he understands very well the way this game goes.' When the priest was winning Voltaire would overturn the board. ' Imagine spending two hours in moving little bits of wood to and fro ! ' he exclaimed. ' One could have written an act of a tragedy in the time.' When he himself was winning, he would play the game out.

It was the Father who said his Mass, for one of Voltaire's first acts at Ferney was to build a church there. Over its porch was put the proud inscription : *Deo Erexit Voltaire*. ' Two great names,' remarked the visitors. Voltaire had also had constructed a tomb for himself, half inside the church and half in the grave-yard. 'The rascals,' he explained, 'will say that I'm neither in nor out.' He had also built a room for stage performances. 'If you meet any of the devout, tell them I've built a church ; if you meet pleasant people, tell them I've finished a theatre.'

Two young girls successively rejuvenated the château. The first was a niece of Corneille, garnered by Voltaire in memory of the poet. To dower her he composed a commentary on Corneille's plays, which was sold for her benefit, and in the end he married her to a certain M. Dupuits. The second was Mlle. de Vari-court, a girl of noble family, but poor, pleasant, and 'of very agreeable plumpness.' 'Delle et Bonne ' was Voltaire's name for her. ' You put me in good humour with myself,' he said : ' I can't be angry in front of you.' When she entered his room of a morning he would call out to her : ' Good morning, good nature ! ' —' Good morning, protecting deity ! ' she answered, and embraced him.—' Ah, made-moiselle,' he exclaimed, ' this is life and death embracing ! ' But death had no distaste for these contacts. Later he married her to the Marquis de Villette, and she always remained devoted to him.

As at Les Délices, his existence at Ferney was extremely active. His work was not entirely literary. He kept building and planting, 'the only activities,' he said, 'which can comfort old age.' His lands fed the thirty people and the twelve horses of the household. From morning to night (he rose at five and went to bed at ten), he busied himself with his agricultural undertakings, or with his stud-farm (he made ill-starred attempts at improving the breed of horses) ; he received countless visitors who presented themselves at his door ; he wrote and dictated voluminous correspondence, pamphlets, tales, plays. Of an evening they would play games to test the wits, or else tell stories of robbers : 'Mesdames,' began M. de Voltaire, 'once upon a time there was a tax-farmer. . . . Good gracious, I've forgotten the rest !' Everything amused him. The only denizens of Ferney whom he found intolerable were the oxen. 'I have quarrelled with the oxen, they walk too slowly. It doesn't suit my vivacity. They're always ailing. I want people who plough fast and are always well.'

For his own part, he was in poor health and hurried through hundreds of things. 'Life is a small thing,' he wrote to Mme. du Deffand, 'enjoy it while you await death, which is a great one.' And to d'Alembert he wrote: 'Walk ever on the path of truth—with a sneer.' Possibly he did good with a sneer, but he certainly did good. The village of Ferney was transformed under his hands to a thriving little town. He cleared land. He built houses for the workers on the land and let them have homes on very easy terms. 'I have left abundance where there was want before. True, only by ruining myself, but a man could not ruin himself in a more decent cause.'

To people his town he took advantage of certain persecutions then proceeding in Geneva. He set up workshops to make silk stockings, and sent the first pair to the Duchesse de Choiseul: 'Deign, madame, but once to slip them on, and then display your legs to whomsoever you choose.' He established a lace-making industry. Above all, he attracted to his seat excellent watchmakers, and took as

much trouble to market the watches of his
subjects as to administer an empire. He re-
commended the Ferney watches to all his
friends in Paris : ' They make them much
better here than at Geneva. . . . For eighteen
louis you will get an excellent repeater here
which would cost you forty in Paris. Send
your orders and they will be fulfilled. . . .
You shall have splendid watches and very bad
verses, whenever you fancy.'

Under the protection of M. de Choiseul he
sent out a circular to the ambassadors of
France at foreign Courts, begging them to re-
commend the watchmakers of Ferney. ' They
merit Your Excellency's protection the more
because they have great respect for the Catholic
religion.' When his friend the Empress of
Russia was waging war against the Turks,
he counted on securing through her the right
of supplying watches for the Greek Church,
but at the same time he was in touch with the
Sultan, to furnish watches to the Turks. In
fine, he had made Ferney into a small paradise,
active and cheerful, and all the happier because
its religious toleration was perfect : ' in my
hamlet, where I have made more than a

hundred Genevese and their families at home, nobody notices that there are two religions.'

Age only augmented his craving for activity and his zest in work : ' the further I advance along the path of life,' he wrote, ' the more do I find work a necessity. In the long run it becomes the greatest of pleasures, and it replaces all one's lost illusions.' And again : ' Neither my old age nor my illnesses dishearten me. Had I cleared but one field and made but twenty trees to flourish, that would still be an imperishable boon.' The philosophy of *Candide* is drawing near.

XV

VOLTAIRE'S PHILOSOPHY

LEGEND is not wrong in seeing the Voltaire of Ferney as the true Voltaire. Before Ferney, what was he ? A very famous poet and playwright, a much-discussed historian, a populariser of science : France regarded him as a brilliant writer, not as an intellectual force. It was Ferney that freed him, and so made him great. Under cover of his quadrilateral of ' dens,' he was now to have the daring to say everything. The battle for freedom of thought which his friends the Encyclopaedists had engaged upon, and could not carry on in Paris without danger, was to be directed by him from his retreat. To that struggle he contributed wit and fancy, an infinite variety in forms, a deliberate uniformity in ideas.

For twenty years Ferney discharged over Europe a hail of pamphlets printed under scores of names, forbidden, confiscated, disowned, denied, but hawked, read, admired, and digested by all the thinking heads of that time. Voltaire at Ferney was no longer the 'fashionable man'; he was a Benedictine of rationalism. He believed in his apostolic mission : ' I have done more in my own time,' he said, ' than Luther and Calvin.' And further : ' I am tired of hearing it declared that twelve men sufficed to establish Christianity, and I want to prove to them that it only needs one to destroy it.' Nearly all his letters ended with the famous formula : ' *Ecrasons l'infâme* '—' We must crush the vile thing ' —or, as he wrote it with ingenuous caution, ' *Ecr. l'inf.*' What was the vile thing ? Religion ? The Church ? To be more exact, it was Superstition. He hounded it down because he had suffered from it, and because he believed that bigotry makes men more unhappy than they need be.

A great part of Voltaire's work at Ferney, then, was destructive. He wanted to show : (*a*) that it is absurd to suppose that an omnipotent God, creator of Heaven and Earth, had chosen the Jews, a small tribe of Bedouin nomads, as His chosen people ; (*b*) that the chronicles of that race (the Bible) was packed with incredible facts, obscenities, and contradictions (he took the trouble to publish under the title of *La Bible Expliquée*, a survey of the biblical text with countless notes) ; (*c*) that the Gospels, although more moral than the Old Testament, were nevertheless full of the gossipings of illiterate nobodies ; and finally (*d*) that the disputes which set the sects at each other's throats throughout eighteen centuries were foolish and unavailing.

The Voltairean criticism has been itself criticised. It has been said that Voltaire lacks sympathy and proportion, and that in any case his own historical science was often at fault. But we must be fair. Voltaire often made particular effort to be so himself. ' It cannot be too often repeated,' he said, ' that we must not judge these centuries by the measure of our own, nor the Jews by that of Frenchmen or Englishmen.' If we are prepared to view the Bible as a collection of legends compiled by barbarian tribes, then he is prepared to admit that it is ' as captivating as Homer.' If we claim to find therein a divine utterance and superhuman thoughts, then he claims the right to quote the prophets, and show their cruel savagery.

What is Voltaire's positive philosophy? It is an agnosticism tempered by a deism. 'It is natural to admit the existence of a God as soon as one opens one's eyes. . . . The creation betokens the Creator. It is by virtue of an admirable art that all the planets dance round the sun. Animals, vegetables, minerals—everything is ordered with proportion, number, movement. Nobody can doubt that a painted landscape or drawn animals are works of skilled artists. Could copies possibly spring from an intelligence and the originals not?'

Regarding the nature of God he has little to teach us. 'Fanatics tell us: God came at such-and-such a time; in a certain small town God preached, and He hardened the hearts of His listeners so that they might have no faith in Him; He spoke to them and they stopped their ears. Now, the whole world should laugh at these fanatics. I shall say as much of all the gods that have been invented. I shall be no more merciful to the monsters of the Indies than to the monsters of Egypt. I shall blame every nation that has abandoned the universal God for all these phantoms of private gods.'

What, then, is to be believed ? That is rather vague. 'The great name of theist is the only one that should be borne ; the only book that should be read is the great book of nature. The sole religion is to worship God and to be an honourable man. This pure and everlasting religion cannot possibly produce harm.' And certainly it would seem difficult for this theism to produce harm ; but is it capable of producing much good ? It is incomprehensible how so hollow and abstract a belief will maintain the weight of a moral system, and the moral system of Voltaire is not actually based on his theism. It is a purely human morality.

A theist in name, a humanist in fact—that is Voltaire. When he wishes seriously to justify a moral precept, he does so through the idea of society. Moreover, as God is everywhere, morality is in nature itself. 'There is something of divinity in a flea.' At all times and in all places man has found a single morality in his own heart. Socrates, Jesus, and Confucius have differing metaphysics, but more or less the same moral system. Replying to Pascal, who found it ' pleasing ' that men such as robbers, who have renounced all the laws of God, should contrive other laws which they scrupulously obey, Voltaire wrote : ' That is more useful than pleasing to consider, for it proves that no society can live for a single day without laws. In this all societies are like games : without rules, they do not exist.' Here the historian has seen aright, and with a penetrating phrase has pointed out what modern observers of primitive societies have since described.

Stern judgment has been passed on this Voltairean philosophy. Faguet defined it as ' a chaos of clear ideas ' ; Taine remarked that ' he dwarfed great things by dint of bringing them within reach ' ; and a woman once said : ' What I cannot forgive him, is having made me understand so many things which I shall never understand.' It is certain that a system imbued with perfect clarity has few chances of being a truthful image of an obscure and mysterious world. But still, it remains probable that this world is in part intelligible, for otherwise there would be neither physics nor mechanics.

Voltaire himself indicated better than any one the limitations of clarity, and how much madness and confusion there are in human destinies. Let doubters turn back to the second part of the article on ' Ignorance ' in the *Philosophical Dictionary* : ' I am ignorant of how I was formed and how I was born. Through a quarter of my lifetime I was absolutely ignorant of the reasons for everything I saw and heard and felt, and was merely a parrot prompted by other parrots. . . . When I sought to advance along that infinite course, I could neither find one single footpath nor fully discover one single object, and from the upward leap I made to contemplate eternity I fell back into the abyss of my ignorance.' Here Voltaire touched hands with Pascal, but only half-way ; and this troubled Voltaire is the best Voltaire, for he is the Voltaire of *Candide*.

XVI

CANDIDE

THE author of *Zaïre* and the *Henriade* would doubtless have been prodigiously surprised had he been assured that the only book (or nearly the only book) of his which would be read in 1950, and held as a masterpiece of man's wit, would be a short novel written at the age of sixty-five, and bearing the title of *Candide*.

He wrote it to ridicule the optimism of Leibniz. ' Everything is for the best in the best of worlds . . .' said the optimists. Voltaire had observed men's lives ; he had lived, battled, suffered, and seen suffering. No, emphatically: this world of stakes and scaffolds, battles and disease, was not the best of possible worlds. Some historians—Michelet especially—have attributed the pessimism of *Candide* to particular occurrences : the dreadful earthquake at Lisbon (on which Voltaire wrote a poem), or the Seven Years' War and its victims, or the greed of Mme. Denis. These petty reasons seem useless. Voltaire denied the perfection of the world because, to an intelligent old man, it did not look perfect.

His theme was simple. It was a novel of apprenticeship, that is, the shaping of an adolescent's ideas by rude contact with the universe. Candide learned to know armies and the Jesuits of Paraguay ; murder, theft, and rape ; France, England, and the Grand Turk. Everywhere his observation showed him that man was rather a wicked animal. Optimist philosophy was personified in Pangloss ; pessimism, in Martin, who thinks that man ' is born to live amid the convulsions of anxiety and the lethargy of ennui.' But the author accepted neither Martin's pessimism nor Pangloss's optimism at their face values. The last words of the book were : ' We must cultivate our garden ' ; that is to say : the world is mad and cruel ; the earth trembles and the sky hurls thunderbolts ; Kings fight and Churches rend each other. Let us limit our activity and try to do as well as we can the small task that seems to be within our powers.

It is, as René Berthelot remarks, an eminently

scientific and bourgeois conclusion. Action is necessary. All is not well, but all things can be bettered. Man ' cannot obliterate the cruelty of the universe, but by prudence he can shield certain small confines from that cruelty.' What Voltaire sets up against Martin's pessimism and Pangloss's optimism, what he opposes to Christian theology and to the stoic optimism resumed by Leibniz, is Newtonian science, the science that limits itself to nature, that makes us grasp only certain connexions, but at least assures us thereby of our power over certain natural phenomena.

No work shows better than *Candide* how fully Voltaire remains a great classic and a man of the eighteenth century, while Rousseau is already a romantic and a man of the nineteenth. Nothing would have been easier than to make *Candide* into a *Childe Harold*. Let Candide take on the semblance of a projection of Voltaire's own personality, let him accuse the Universe of having robbed him of Mademoiselle Cunégonde, let him conceive of a personal struggle between himself and Destiny—and he would be a romantic hero. But Candide is universal as a character of Molière's is universal, and it was the reading of *Candide* that shaped the second Byron, the anti-romantic, the Byron of *Don Juan*. That is why all romantics are anti-Voltairean, even Michelet, whose political fervour ought to have made him stand aligned with Voltaire, and that is why, on the other hand, all the minds which accept the world and recognise its irony and indifference are Voltairean. M. Jacques Bainville has said that M. Charles Maurras re-reads his *Candide* once a year, and as he closes it, says to himself : ' The road is clear '—' that is to say, that Voltaire sweeps earthly illusions boldly aside, drives away the clouds and all that is interposed between reality and understanding.'

One reason for the enduring success of *Candide* is that it represents one of the attitudes of the human mind, and perhaps the bravest. But above all, it is admirable as a work of art. Alain has justly observed that the style of *Candide* resembles that of the *Arabian Nights* in Galland's translation. The union of classic French, proving and deducing consequences with such clarity, and the fantastic image of life formed by the fatalist Orient, was bound to produce a novel dissonance, and did in fact produce one. The poetry of a text is largely produced by the fact that the wild chaos of the universe are therein, at one and the same time, expressed and controlled by a rhythm. In *Candide* both characteristics exist. Over every page stream unforeseeable cascades of facts, and yet the swift movement, the regular recurrence of the optimist themes of Pangloss, the pessimist themes of Martin, the narratives of the old woman and the refrains of Candide, afford the mind that troubled, tragic repose which is only given by great poetry.

Alongside the Galland influence, that of Swift should be noted. Voltaire had read much of Swift, and was fond of him ; and from the Dean he had learned how to tell an absurd story in the most natural manner. Of all the classic French texts, *Candide* is certainly the most closely akin to the English humorists. But Swift's rather fierce humour, sometimes too emphatic, is here tempered by the desire to please. In the body of every writer's creation there are things of sheer delight : *Candide* was the best of such in Voltaire's.

XVII

MINOR WORKS

VOLTAIRE worked hard at Ferney, producing there the most important part of his work. It was there that he completed the great labours started at Cirey and at Potsdam : the *Essay on Morals*, the history of *Russia under Peter the Great*, and the *Philosophical Dictionary*. Of the *Essay on Morals* we have already spoken ; the *Dictionary* is a collection of notes arranged alphabetically, unified only by its underlying doctrine. The idea had been suggested to Voltaire during a supper-party with Frederick the Great ; it was bound to attract a man who enjoyed talking of everything and had no love for ' composing ' in the formal seventeenth-century sense.

There is in existence a history of French clarity ; it would be instructive to sketch a history of the French vagary and of uncomposed works, which would bring together Montaigne's *Essays*, the *Characters* of La Bruyère,

Voltaire's *Dictionary*, and the *Analecta* of Paul
Valéry. The *Essay on Morals* itself is only a
kind of encyclopaedia with articles ranged in
chronological order. The dictionary form suited
Voltaire so well that he fell back upon it several
times. In 1764 a first volume appeared, which
was seized and publicly burnt. Then came the
Questions touching the Encyclopaedia, and lastly the
Alphabetic Opinion. After Voltaire's death the
whole was merged into the *Philosophical Dictionary* of the Kehl edition, containing anecdotes, theology, science, history, music, verse,
and dialogues.

At Ferney, too, Voltaire wrote numerous
philosophic tales, and several of these, although
falling short of the perfection of *Candide*, are
amusing and penetrating. *Jeannot and Colin*
should be read, a pleasing and ingenuous
satire on the wealthy; *The Man with Forty
Crowns*, too, an economic pamphlet rather than
a novel; the *History of Jenni*, which has an
opening chapter in the best Voltaire vein;
and then *The Simpleton*, the *Princess of Babylon*,
The White Bull, and lastly, *White and Black*,
which has something of the poetry of *Candide*
without its full power.

But the greater part of this mass of work is composed of pamphlets, small books and dialogues, which made Voltaire (along with Addison) the greatest journalist whom men have known. To set forth his ideas and make game of the ideas of his opponents, he created a whole race of puppets : there were the letters of a Hindu victim of the Inquisitors (the *Letters of Amabed*), the theological inquiries of a Spanish licentiate (the *Questions of Zapata*), the advice of the guardian of the Ragusa Capucins to Brother Pediculoso on his setting forth for the Holy Land—' the first thing you will do, Brother Pediculoso, is to go and see the earthly paradise where God created Adam and Eve, so familiar to the ancient Greeks and early Romans, to the Persians, Egyptians, and Syrians, that none of them ever mentioned it. . . . You need only ask the way of the Capucins in Jerusalem ; you can't get lost.' There is the canonisation of Saint Cucufin, brother of Ascoli, by Pope Clement XIII., and his miraculous appearance to Monsieur Avelin, citizen of Troyes. There is the sermon of Rabbi Akib, and a rescript of the Emperor of China, and the journey of Brother

Garassise, poisoned by the journal of the Jesuits and saved by fragments of the *Encyclopaedia*, which dissolve for him in a little white wine.

Wit sometimes fails this polemical literature. The *Canonisation of Saint Cucufin* is a clumsy and humourless joke. But the contemporary reader was certain to be delighted by the movement and the intoxicating rhythm of most of these fantasies, their gaiety, their glittering style, and above all by their topical quality. And the contemporary could appreciate more than we can the courage of the polemist. For all his stature and his strongholds, he was still menaced from time to time. Queen Maria Lecszinska, on her deathbed, asked that his impiousness be punished. 'What can I do, madame?' answered the King. 'If he were in Paris I should exile him to Ferney.' Less reasonable than the sovereign, the Parlement ordered the burning of the *Man with Forty Crowns*, and pilloried a luckless bookseller who had sold a copy. When the case was called, one of the magistrates exclaimed in the criminal court: 'Is it only his books we shall burn?' Notwithstanding the proximity of the frontier, Voltaire was often seized by panic, but he could not resist his demon.

Candide, the tales, and the *Century of Louis XIV* are beyond doubt Voltaire's masterpieces, but in order to understand why and how he exercised so wide an influence over the France of his time, it is necessary to skim his numerous topical writings, ephemeral in subject but not in form, and to imagine what power over opinion was wielded by this journalist of genius, who, tirelessly handling the same themes, was able to astound, excite, and dominate France for over twenty years.

XVIII

THE CASE OF CALAS

ABOUT the end of March 1762, a traveller coming from Languedoc called at Ferney, and told Voltaire about a criminal prosecution which had been stirring the citizens of Toulouse. Jean Calas, a Protestant shopkeeper very highly respected in the town, had just been sent to the scaffold for the murder of his son in the following circumstances.

Marc-Antoine Calas, one of his sons, a young fellow of somewhat gloomy temperament, had for some time shown signs of melancholia. He could no longer carry on his studies for a legal career because he was a Protestant, and at the same time was unwilling to be a merchant like his father. His favourite reading was *Hamlet*, and Seneca's pages on suicide.

On October 13th, 1761, when the family were entertaining a friend, he rose from table before the others and went into the kitchen, where the servant said to him : ' Come near the fire.' —' I'm burning ! ' he exclaimed in answer, and thereupon went down to the warehouse. Soon after this the friend wished to leave ; the second son held a light for him to pass through the shop, and discovered his brother hanging from the folding door, dead. He called out ; the father and mother hurried down. The rope was cut. Neighbours arrived, and in an instant some bigot was insisting that Marc-Antoine had been done to death by his own family, that he had wanted to become a Catholic, that he was to make his recantation next day, and that it was a rule amongst the Protestants that a father should prefer his child's death to his recantation.

The accusation was absurd ; this so-called rule had never existed. Every one acquainted with the life of the Calas family testified to the fondness and kindness of the father. One of his sons, Louis, had been converted shortly before, under the influence of a Catholic servant : Calas had forgiven his son, and even kept the servant. And besides, how could an old man have been able to master and hang a vigorous and resisting youth! The complicity of the whole family and their guest would have been essential. Can one imagine a father, mother, and brothers, all assembled to kill one of themselves? In any case, there was no serious evidence to show that the victim had been desirous of becoming converted. But the case came before an excitable magistrate. The pious joined in. A solemn service was held for Marc-Antoine in a church swathed in white, in the middle of which was suspended a skeleton lent by a surgeon. The skeleton held in one hand a paper inscribed ' *Recantation of Heresy*,' and in the other a palm, emblematic of martyrdom.

The affair came before the Parlement of Toulouse. All the members of the Calas family were arrested, and separately interrogated. All maintained the truth of their first account of events. By eight votes to five the father was condemned to be broken on the wheel, his son, Pierre, was banished, and the others set free. It was a judgment as foolish as it was cruel, because either the whole family were accomplices, or they were all innocent. Old Calas bore the horrors of the examination with admirable constancy. Questioned about his accomplices he kept repeating : ' Alas ! How can there be accomplices where there is no crime ? '

In the end he was put to death. The executioner shattered the bones of his limbs and chest with blows of an iron bar. Then he was bound to the wheel, to die slowly and then be burnt. To the priest beside him he said : ' I die innocent. Jesus Christ, Who was innocence itself, was willing to perish by still more cruel punishments. I have no regrets for a life whose end, I trust, will lead me to eternal joys. I mourn for my wife and my son ; and that poor stranger to whom I thought I was doing a kindness in bidding him to supper, makes me the more sorry still. . . .' The Catholic priests present had no doubts of his innocence, and said that, Protestant though he was, he died like a martyr.

The story amazed Voltaire. The crime struck him as most unlikely, but he could not believe in such malevolence amongst the magistrates of Toulouse. It happened that some of the Calas family had sought refuge in Geneva, not far from Ferney; he had them brought out, and after questioning them several times was fully convinced of their innocence. From that moment, throughout four years, the rehabilitation of the Calas family became his main preoccupation. He interested the Duc de Choiseul in their cause. The King of Prussia and the Empress of Russia, started off by him, agitated on behalf of the Calases. All Europe took sides, to such effect that in the end Voltaire secured a revision of the trial, ' notwithstanding a few devout persons who openly maintained that it was better to let an innocent old Calvinist be broken on the wheel than to let eight councillors of the province be exposed to the risk of agreeing that they had been mistaken. There was even some who said : *There are more magistrates than Calases*, arguing therefrom that the Calas family should be immolated in honour of the magistracy. It was not realised that the honour of judges is dependent, like that of other men, on their righting of what they have done wrong.'

The Parlement of Paris took over the case, and behaved well in the matter. In the spring of 1766 the Toulouse decision was quashed, and it was a day of festivity in Paris. ' Crowds gathered in the public squares. Men hastened to set eyes on this hapless and now fully vindicated family. Applause greeted the judges as they passed by, and blessings were poured on their heads. The spectacle was made all the more affecting by the fact that that very day, March 9th, was the day on which, three years before, Calas had died under the most cruel torture.' The King granted 36,000 *livres* as compensation to the unfortunate widow, and Voltaire wrote a *Treatise on Tolerance* to demonstrate that *every man has the right to hold and express whatever opinion seems right to him, provided that he does not trouble public order*. ' If you would be like Jesus Christ,' he concluded, ' be martyrs and not executioners.'

Elementary truths : but they were truths which it was necessary to repeat, and even, as he said, to hammer home again and again, so long as a Calas affair was a possibility. This case, and that of the Sirvens, another Protestant family in Toulouse, accused of an almost identical crime and likewise defended by Voltaire, did more for his popular fame than his writings. Thirty years later the National Convention decreed that there should be erected at the Republic's expense, ' on the square where Calas was slain by fanaticism,' a marble column bearing the inscription :

THE NATIONAL CONVENTION :

TO

PATERNAL LOVE

TO

NATURE

TO

CALAS, VICTIM OF FANATICISM.

That came to pass in the year 1793, when the same assembly cut off the heads of many hundreds of Frenchmen who did not share its views.

XIX

THE CHEVALIER DE LA BARRE

' In Abbeville, a small town in Picardy, there lived an abbess of kindly nature and sober habit of life.' She was paid court to by a citizen of the town named Belleval, a man of sixty and lieutenant of a petty local tribunal. She gently rebuffed him.

In 1764 this abbess gave hospitality to a nephew of hers, the Chevalier de la Barre, a young man of nineteen, who lodged outside the convent house, but frequently came thither to sup with some of his friends. M. Belleval, who had not been brought into these supper-parties and had conceived a deep resentment against the abbess, knew that young La Barre and a friend of his, the son of the Président d'Etal-londes, had passed close to a religious procession without baring their heads, and from that moment strove to have ' this forgetfulness of good manners regarded as a premeditated insult

126

to religion. A few days later a wooden crucifix placed on the old bridge at Abbeville was found damaged one morning. It had probably been knocked by a passing cart during the night, but the incident was distorted into a wilful mutilation and sacrilege. The Bishop of Amiens came in solemn procession, and these occurrences became the general talk of Abbeville.

Belleval mischievously confounded the affair of the crucifix with that of the procession, and began probing into the private life of the Chevalier de la Barre. He obtained against the youth a Monitory, that is to say, an episcopal letter publicly read from the pulpit, obliging the faithful under pain of excommunication to give testimony concerning the said facts. Nothing could be more dangerous, for a publicly stated suspicion always gives rise to false witness. The world contains only too many foolish and mischievous people, and any excitement gives them full rein. A witness was found to state that La Barre had sung improper songs, another to swear that he had employed a gross expression in referring to Saint Mary Magdalen, a third to report facts of equal gravity. This was all that could be proved, and that only by uncorroborated evidence denied by the accused.

The judges of Abbeville, however, with inconceivable cruelty, condemned young d'Etallondes, aged eighteen years, to have his tongue cut out at the root, his right hand cut off at the door of the principal church, and to be then tied to a stake and burnt on a slow fire. Fortunately the youth had taken flight. But the Chevalier de la Barre was in their grasp. 'The judges, in his favour, had the humanity to soften the sentence by ordering that he should be beheaded before being burnt. This astounding sentence was carried out on February 28th, 1766.'

La Barre was conveyed to Paris. The Procureur-Général was in favour of quashing the sentence of the Abbeville court, but it was confirmed by fifteen judges against ten. This time the whole of France regarded the sentence with horror. The Chevalier de la Barre was sent back to Abbeville for execution. The Dominican who attended him during the torture, at the sight of his sufferings, was unable to eat. 'We must take some nourishment,' said the Chevalier to him. 'You will need as much strength as I shall to stand the spectacle I am going to provide.' All that he said before the punishment was : ' I did not think they could put a young gentleman to death for such a trifle.' When the news of his death reached Paris, the Nuncio publicly stated that he would not have been treated thus in Rome. On the same bonfire as the Chevalier there was burnt the *Philosophical Dictionary* of Voltaire.

Such horrors tore Voltaire from his irony and titterings. For over ten years he sought the rehabilitation of M. d'Etallondes and harried the judges of La Barre. He did not succeed.

Judicial errors belong to all ages, but at that time they seem to have been particularly serious. After the Calas affair nearly all of them were referred to Ferney. In 1766 Voltaire defended the memory of the Comte de Lolly-Tollendal, beheaded after the loss of the Indies for betrayal of the King's interests, and succeeded in rehabilitating that unjustly condemned officer. In 1769 he rehabilitated a farmer named Martin, broken on the wheel for a crime subsequently admitted by the real culprit. In 1770 there was the trial of the Montbaillis, husband and wife, of Saint Omer; unfortunately Voltaire

was only able to intervene after the unjust
execution of the husband, but he had the wife
absolved.   Sometimes he himself made mis-
takes and defended the guilty ; but it was better
to acquit a culprit than to torture the innocent.
In the fiscal field he did a great service to the
peasantry of the Pays de Gex, amongst whom
he lived, by freeing them from the mortmain
and salt-tax.   When the three Orders of Gex
met to approve the agreement reached with
France, the ceremony was presided over by
Voltaire, who appeared at the window and
called out : ' Liberty ! '—' Long live the King !
Long live Voltaire ! ' cried the crowd.

' With him,' wrote Mme. de Gallatin, ' were
twelve dragoons from Ferney who were stationed
on the space in front of the house where the
assembly was held. . . . The twelve dragoons
presented arms in honour of our friend, who
left at once and was back in time for dinner.
Laurels were flung into his carriage as he
passed through several villages. He was covered
with them.   All his subjects were lined up to
greet him, saluting him with a salvo of boxes,
pots and pans, etc. . . . He was delighted, and
did not notice his eighty-two years.'

XX

THE PATRIARCH

IT is an added strength for a celebrated writer
to live to be old. He thereby gains the affection of the crowd, who, though ignorant of his
work, admire his longevity ; he wins the in-
dulgence of his juniors, who, fairly certain of
seeing him shortly disappear, find the courage
to do him justice ; and he reaches that freedom
of mind natural to a man who sees himself not
far from annihilation or judgment, according
to his beliefs, and is so able to resume, if he
has not always retained it, his habit of free
speech on the affairs of this world. Voltaire
after 1764, aged seventy and then eighty,
became the patriarch of intelligent Europe.
He was treated no longer as a man but as a
symbol, and if the Bishop of Annecy denounced
him to the Court for an improper and un-
dignified trick which he played in order to
receive the Blessed Sacrament—the Minister,

who in days gone by would have imprisoned him, did no more than address him a letter in slightly stern tones. 'There are only three great men left in Europe,' said Vestris the dancer, 'the King of Prussia, Voltaire, and myself.'

All monarchs, except his own, treated him as a spiritual power. When his friends in Paris wished to raise a statue to him, four crowned heads subscribed : the Emperor of Russia, and the Kings of Prussia, Poland, and Denmark. He was pleased. 'Four kings in my hand !' he exclaimed. 'I must win the rubber ! Isn't it wonderful how this life is made up of mixed high cards and low, black and white, and don't you feel annoyed that there is not one from the South amongst my four Kings ? '

Frederick had turned back to him after five years of estrangement and silence. 'A lover's quarrel,' said Voltaire. 'Court squabbles blow over, but the character of a noble ruling passion endures for a long time.' Correspondence had been resumed, a little stiffly at first, because Prussia was at war with France. But patriotism in those days was a less jealous sentiment

than now, and verse epistles could then be
bandied across the lines of battle which to-day
would cause a terrible scandal. From Frederick
came the lines :

> Delightful madmen, charming race,
> Who prate of peace and never make it :
> Resolve at last, O Janus face !
> For Peace or War—how will ye take it ?

And Voltaire replied :

> Master of Arts in verse and arms,
> Of skill in both you show no dearth :
> So pen your rhymes, and brave alarms,
> Teach men, and ravage all their earth !
> Verses I love and war I hate,
> Yet all your frenzied martial state
> I'll not oppose : for every mind
> Must take the colour of its kind.
> 'Tis clear, say I,
> What pleasures lie
> In mastering thus the sister arts
> Of slaying men and winning hearts.

It is less clear to us. And Frederick concluded that : ' it is for M. Martin and Doctor
Pangloss to discuss this matter, and for myself to
fight as long as there is fighting. You yourself
are a spectator of the bloody drama we are playing, and you can hiss all of us for what we are.'

The relationship between the two men had altered ; their letters were more frank, their epithets less fulsome : 'Your soldier's calling and your position as King do not make your heart very sensitive,' wrote Voltaire bitterly ; and Frederick, at the time of the La Barre case, set up reasons of State against Voltaire's : 'Is it necessary to batter against prejudices which time has consecrated ? Do you remember that remark of Fontenelle ? He said : *If I had my hand full of truths I should think more than once before opening it.*' These things said, the two men admired each other. And later, when Frederick had outlived Voltaire, he was not to forget him : 'I say a prayer to him every morning. *Divine Voltaire*, I say, *pray for us.*'

Another 'enlightened' and warlike sovereign had become a friend of the patriarch— Catherine the Great. Their correspondence had begun apropos of the life of Peter the Great, which Voltaire had written, and at once took on a tone of respectful familiarity, Catherine praising Voltaire for his defence of Calas, Voltaire praising Catherine for causing 'reason, innocence, and virtue' to triumph in her dominions. There was a long sentimental passage between them regarding the war with Turkey : ' I admit that in spite of the war my village has despatched cases of watches for Constantinople. Thus I am in correspondence at once with victors and vanquished. I do not yet know whether Mustapha has bought any of my watches, but I do know that he missed the moment of a charming hour with you, and that more than once you gave him a bad quarter-of-an-hour.'

It is hard to say whether Voltaire found mental pleasure in these royal friendships, but he certainly found in them the pleasures of vanity. To such heights did the sense of his own intellectual majesty actually rise that he felt decidedly affronted when the Emperor Joseph II., passing through Geneva, did not come out to Ferney like everybody else.

The number of visitors waxed with the years. D'Alembert came, and was charmed. The Chevalier d'Etallondes, the surviving hero of the unhappy Abbeville affair, was welcomed with emotion. But Voltaire was always pressed with work, and shunned the ordinary traveller. These arrived every day—artists, savants, philosophers, German princes, Polish princes, Russian princes. He got rid of them by manipulating his old weapon—his health : ' Quick, quick ! Send for Tronchin . . .' he would say, referring to his physician. ' You see a dying man before you, I have but a few moments to live. . . .' He was crippled, deaf, and almost blind. The next moment he was leaping with a child's lightness to uproot a weed from his borders which he had seen from ten feet away.

All the visitors have described his cadaverous appearance. He himself, when Pigalle was anxious to make his statue, remarked : ' M. Pigalle is to come and model my face. But, madame, I must *have* a face ! You can barely imagine its position. My eyes have sunk three inches ; my cheeks are old parchment badly gummed on to bones that have nothing to hold to ; the few teeth I had are gone. Nobody has ever carved a poor creature in such a state.' The ' poor creature ' recovered all his mental nimbleness to extract from the sculptor an argument in favour of his pet thesis. He asked Pigalle how long it would take to carve a horse three feet in height, and made him sign a declaration : 'I require six months.' An instant triumph—how could Aaron in the Bible have been able to make the Golden Calf *in one night* ? During his few remaining years he was constantly to set up Pigalle against the defenders of the ' sacred text.'

Having once found such a topic he would shut himself up, and spend a day and a night in the composition of an article for the *Philosophical Dictionary*, or a dialogue, or a pamphlet. Next day would find him worn out. But how could he stop being busy, writing, constructing, battling, taking risks ? ' Life is a child that must be rocked till it falls asleep.' He was an invalid. He always had been. For eight years he had been an invalid. For eighty years he had had only a moment to live, and that moment was ended. He was dying. Perhaps he was even dead. ' He has forgotten to have himself buried,' said one visitor.

XXI

THE CORONATION OF VOLTAIRE

Why did an old man of eighty-three decide to undertake the long and dangerous journey from Ferney to Paris ? ' I—I, go to Paris ? ' he exclaimed. ' Do they know that there are forty thousand bigots in that city, who would call down blessings from heaven and carry faggots to heap round the stake for me ? '—' But,' answered the friend who encouraged him to make the journey, ' do you know that you have eighty thousand friends there who would all rush to put out the fire, and, if it amused you, drown the faggot-bearers ? '

During the lifetime of Louis xv. his return had been forbidden. On the accession of Louis xvi. all the Ministers were changed ; ' enlightened and virtuous ' men like Malesherbes and Turgot were summoned to their places, and Paris was now open to Voltaire. The women of the household, Mme. Denis and

Mme. de Villette, urged him to go. In Paris the Encyclopaedist group desired the journey to be made. Moreover, Voltaire had just written a tragedy, *Irène*, which he intended for the Comédie-Française. The actors were falling out, and *Irène* would suffer in consequence. The octogenarian had its success deeply at heart. He imagined that his presence would put everything right. He set off.

He went through the village of Ferney, assuring his weeping villagers that he would be back in six weeks' time. He too was in tears, and then, when he had passed the last house, became very cheerful and started off on endless stories. At Bourg he was recognised by the crowd, and the postmaster gave him his best horses, saying to the postillion: 'Fast as you can, lad; drive 'em till they drop—I don't care: you're driving M. de Voltaire.' At Dijon some young men of the town disguised themselves as footmen to serve him. At the barrier of Paris the officials recognised him: 'M. de Voltaire,' and bowed respectfully, only venturing to ask whether he had anything dutiable with him. Soon afterwards he reached the corner of the Rue de Beaune and what is

now called the Quai Voltaire, at the house of
Mme. de Villette. And immediately, ' in a
periwig of the Regency period crowned with a
red velvet cap trimmed with fur,' he went to
pay a call on M. d'Argental : ' I have inter-
rupted my death-agony,' he said, ' to come and
shake your hand.'

His arrival excited Paris more than any
sovereign's. He was the sole topic of conversation in resorts and cafés. Men greeted each
other with the enquiry : ' Have you seen him?'
The Hôtel de Villette was crammed with callers.
The Academy sent a deputation. The company of the Comédie-Française came in a body.
Voltaire received in dressing-gown and night-
cap, and then went back to work on revising
Irène. Mme. du Deffand came. Benjamin
Franklin brought his grandson and solicited
Voltaire's blessing for him. The old man
stretched out a hand : ' God and Liberty,'
he said.

The meeting of Franklin and Voltaire, democracy shaking hands with theism, was the
Revolution's dawning. Wherever the two men
appeared together, ' whether at the play or in
public places or at the Academies, applause

was continuous. Voltaire sneezed. 'God bless you, sir!' said Franklin—and the business began again.'[1] Diderot came, and talked to such effect that Voltaire could not get a word in. 'That man has certainly wit,' he remarked, 'but nature has refused him one essential gift— that of dialogue.'[2] Ministers came. The Court was alone in showing him no favour, but did not dare to send him back to Ferney. In the throbbing Paris of those days one rash act would have started an outbreak.

He was being treated like a god, but meanwhile his body thought fit to remind him of his mortality. He was spitting blood. It was suggested to him that a confessor be sent for. Every eye in Paris was on his response; it was ambiguous. He asked to make a public confession, such as was practised in the first centuries of the Church. The Abbé Gauthier refused this, and insisted on a declaration of his religious sentiments. He did not sign it, dismissing the confessor with the words : 'Enough for to-day : we must have no bloodshed on the stage.' His own particular anxiety was for the rehearsals of *Irène*. 'It would be a sad business,'

[1] Mme. d'Epinay.   [2] Bellessort, p. 368.

he said, 'if I had only come to Paris to be confessed and hissed.'

Irène was not hissed, but was a delirious success. To Frederick II. he wrote : 'I have been engaged in avoiding two things which chased me in Paris : booings, and death. I am glad that I have escaped both of these mortal sicknesses, at the age of eighty-four.'

He was not able to be present at the first performance of his tragedy, but on the occasion of the sixth performance, on March 30th, was again well enough to go out. The scene was astounding. Paris went mad. In a blue carriage covered with gold stars the old skeleton in his fur-trimmed velvet coat, with a small cane in his hand, drove through 'his' city. The whole of the Academy, excepting the Bishops, stood on the threshold to welcome him. A dense crowd in the streets shouted : 'Make way for Voltaire !' Guards escorted him as he stepped out of his carriage and accompanied him to his box. On his entry the audience rose to their feet. 'Long live Voltaire !' came the shouts. 'Hail to the defender of Calas ! Hail to the universal man !'

In the end the public insisted on the actors

bringing him a crown. Between the two plays the curtain was raised ; a statue of Voltaire stood upon the stage. All the actors and actresses trooped past the statue, laying laurel wreaths on its head, and each time the crowd, standing up and turning towards Voltaire, shouted : ' The public's offering ! ' Finally the crowd brought him back in triumph to the Hôtel de Villette. Women almost carried him in their arms. ' Do you wish to kill me with happiness, ladies ? ' he said. Never had a writer received such homage. But he kept his head. ' What crowds to greet you ! ' some one said to him.—' Alas ! ' he replied. ' There would be just as many to see me on the scaffold.'

For a few weeks longer he went out and about the conquered city. At home he worked incessantly, saying that he had but a short time to live and must merit the honours which the public had done him. At last, on May 11th, a fever seized him. Tronchin diagnosed a cancer of the prostate. He suffered much pain and became delirious. The accounts of his death are contradictory, each party, the Church and the philosophers, having been eager to make it appear exemplary. The parish priest refused him burial, threatening to have him thrown into the common ditch. And so he was buried outside of Paris, at Sellières, where his nephew was the abbé. His heart was preserved at the Bibliothèque Nationale. It is still there.

XXII

EPILOGUE AND JUDGMENT

LIVES which have made a great stir on earth do not sink at once into the silent sleep of the tomb. The brilliant, dancing *allegretto* of Voltaire's life could not pass abruptly into an *andante maestoso*. For some time longer his royal friends continued to bestir themselves. Frederick II. ordered a bust by Houdon. Catherine was anxious to buy his library, asking this in a letter addressed to Mme. Denis, ' the niece of a great man who loved me a little.'

In France, a Revolution of which he would not have approved (for he was a conservative and monarchist), but for which he had paved the way, treated him as a prophet. In 1791 the Constituent Assembly ordered the transference of Voltaire's ashes to the Panthéon. It was a fine procession, at the head of which went ' Belle et Bonne' weeping, in a Greek robe. In 1814, at the time of the Restoration, the sarcophagus was profaned in circumstances which have remained mysterious. Nobody knows what has become of the frail skeleton and ' the fleshless bones ' which for over eighty years supported with their flimsy framework the noble genius of M. de Voltaire.

Diderot, d'Alembert, and Montesquieu had perhaps played just as great a rôle in the transformation of eighteenth-century France. But Voltaire and Rousseau have remained, both to Frenchmen and to the world in general, the two symbolic figures of that period. Voltaire stands for its satiric and destructive facet, Rousseau for the popular and sentimental facet. Throughout the nineteenth century battles raged round these two names. In that long warfare between Church and State, which ended (if it did end) at the time of the Dreyfus Affair with the victory of the State, Voltaire was the sacred writer of the Church's adversaries. Voltairean became a regular adjective, defined in one famous dictionary as a man who ' has feelings of mocking incredulity regarding Christianity.' M. Homais in Flaubert's *Madame Bovary* was a Voltairean : ' *écrasez l'infâme* ' he kept repeating. Certain critics have treated

Voltaire as if he were merely a M. Homais ;
but others have felt that M. Homais and Voltaire were both necessary, and that Voltaire
even did a service to truly religious minds by
making an abrupt separation of religion and
persecution.

Was his character great ? He was complex.
He laughed at kings and flattered them. To
the Churches he preached forgiveness of insults,
and did not show his own enemies mercy. He
was generous and miserly, frank and untruth-
ful, cowardly and brave. He had the fear of
blows which is natural to human beings, but
all his life long he flung himself into affairs
where he could receive blows. At Ferney he
was like a hare in its form, but a fierce one, a
hare which in the jungle of politics sometimes
held a lion at bay. He had always great difficulty in resisting the bait of a profitable deal,
but still more in abstaining from a dangerous
act of beneficence.

Was his intelligence great ? He was in-
quisitive about everything. He knew more
history than the mathematicians, and more
physics than the historians. He could mould
his genius with ease to very diverse disciplines.

Such universal minds, it may be thought, are not deeply versed in any subject, and ' vulgarisation ' is sometimes mistaken for ' vulgarity,' but that in itself is rather shallow thinking. It is essential that syntheses should be made from time to time, and that inquiring minds should digest the work of the specialists for the benefit of men at large. Failing this, an unbridgable gulf would appear between the expert and the man-in-the-street, and this would be a great anomaly. Besides, ' clarity ' is not synonymous with ' vulgarity,' except perhaps in poetry, and that is why Voltaire is a poet only in his tales, where he laid aside his ' clarity.'

Had he a great heart ? He loathed suffering, for others as for himself, and he helped mankind in the task of avoiding dreadful and useless suffering. A friend once found him reading certain historical topics with tears in his eyes. ' Ah ! ' said Voltaire, ' how wretched men have been, and how much to be pitied ! And they were wretched only because they were cowards and fools.' He was rarely a fool, and never a coward when torture and intolerance had to be fought. ' Yes, I say things over and over again,' he exclaimed. ' That's the privilege of my age, and I'll say them over and over and over again until my fellow-countrymen are cured of their folly.' There may be matter for astonishment that he was not ill-disposed towards war, which is one form of torture, and one of the worst ; but he lived in a time when wars were waged by professional armies, which was a very intelligent method, and a comparatively harmless one.

Why, amongst all the eighteenth-century philosophers, does this quite unphilosophical man stand out as the greatest ? Perhaps it is because that century, at once bourgeois and gentlemanly, universal and frivolous, scientific and fashionable, European and dominantly French, was most fully reflected in the person of Voltaire, who was in himself all of these things.

Add, that he was extremely French, in the sense that other countries use the term. The rest of this planet has always liked in France the writers who, like Voltaire or Anatole France, express simple ideas with clarity, wit, and polish. That particular blend is not the whole of France, but it is part of France, and in the best Frenchmen there is always a little of it present. It was in some measure due to Voltaire that French, in the eighteenth century, was the supreme language of Europe, and the glory of that tongue, coruscating in the mirrors of the European Courts, encircled the old man of Ferney with a startling resplendence.

Finally, and above all else, he was marvellously alive ; and mankind, dreading boredom even more than anxieties, is grateful to those who make life throb with a swifter, stronger beat. In the downpour of pamphlets, epistles, stories, poems, and letters that was showered on France for so many years from Cirey and Berlin and Ferney, there were trivialities and excellences. But everything was swift and bright, and Frenchmen felt their wits coming alive to the tune of M. de Voltaire's fiddling. A graver music some may prefer ; but his must have had charm in plenty, for after more than a century France has not yet wearied of what has been so well called the *prestissimo* of Voltaire.

BIBLIOGRAPHICAL NOTE

FOR quotations the Avenel edition of Voltaire's complete works (published by *Le Siècle*, Paris, 1867, 8 vols.) has been used. This edition includes the introductory Life of Voltaire by Condorcet, and useful notes on the separate works.

Useful memoirs include : *Mémoires sur Voltaire* (Aimé André, Paris, 1826) ; *Les Lettres de Mme. de Graffigny, suivies de celles de Mmes. de Staal, du Boccage, Suard, du Chevalier de Boufflers, du Marquis de Villette, etc.*, edited by Eugène Asse (Charpentier, Paris, 1879) ; and those of Mme. de Staal-Delaunay (for the Life of the Duchesse du Maine).

The principal biography is that by Desnoireterres : *Voltaire et la Société Française au XVIIIe Siècle* (Didier, Paris, 8 vols.). In English may be noted the Lives by John Morley, Richard Aldington, and C. E. Vulliamy.

Amongst numerous critical studies should be noted : *Essais Critiques*, by F. Brunetière ; *Le XVIIIe Siècle*, by E. Faguet (rather unfair) ; the very intelligent notes on Voltaire's novels by J. Bainville,

published by the Cité des Livres, Paris, 1930 ;
Books and Characters, by Lytton Strachey. Cf. also,
Histoire de la Clarté Française, by D. Mornet, *passim*.

Sources for Chapter I : *Ancien Régime*, by Taine ;
Qu'est-ce qu'un Classique ? by Fidao-Justiniani.

INDEX

153